FROM NYET TO DA
*Understanding
the Russians*

The InterAct Series

GEORGE W. RENWICK, Series Editor

FROM NYET TO DA

Understanding the Russians

YALE RICHMOND

INTERCULTURAL PRESS, INC.

For information, contact:
Intercultural Press, Inc.
P.O. Box 700
Yarmouth, Maine 04096, USA

Library of Congress Cataloging-in-Publication Data

Richmond, Yale, 1923-
    From nyet to da: understanding the Russians/Yale Richmond.
        p.   cm. — (InterAct Series)
    Includes bibliographical references and index.
    ISBN 1-877864-08-0: $15.95
    1. Russian S.F.S.R.   I. Title.   II. Title: Understanding the
Russians.   III. Series..
DK510.23.R53   1992
947.085—dc20   91-40331
                                                                       CIP

Contents

To Phyllis, for her encouragement and patience.

I have never met anyone who understood Russians.
—Grand Duke Aleksandr Mikhailovich

Preface

On this continent—and not only on this one—we had since time immemorial been rivals with the Americans. We are now attempting, and not unsuccessfully, to interact.

—Eduard Shevardnadze, April 1990

The Cold War has waned, relations with Russia have warmed, communism has collapsed, and the Soviet Union has been transformed into a Commonwealth of Independent States. Russians are traveling abroad more freely, and Americans are finding that distant land with its new freedoms to be a much more exciting place to visit. Americans and Russians are discovering that they have more to gain from cooperation than confrontation. Citizens of the two countries are interacting, as former Foreign Minister Shevardnadze carefully put it, "not unsuccessfully."

Russia and America remain separated, however, by distance, culture, language, history, and misunderstandings. Joint ventures find willing partners, but "doing business" with Russians is still a challenge.

More than thirty years of cultural, scholarly, and scientific exchanges have made a start in bridging the understanding gap, but Russians and Americans are still puzzled by actions and attitudes that differ from their own. The need for improved understanding remains a challenge on both sides.

There are no shortcuts to understanding the Russians. It helps to know their language, history, and literature, and to have worked with them over the years. But that takes time, and Americans are an impatient people, seeking quick fixes for complex issues.

While not intended as a quick fix, this book has been written for those Americans without previous experience in Russian affairs who will be interacting with Russians in the coming years—students, scholars, scientists, business executives, performing artists, and athletes, as well as ordinary citizens.

The book is based on my more than twenty-five years of working with Russians—negotiating and facilitating people-to-people exchanges in culture, education, and science—when U.S.-Soviet relations were good and when they were not. These years include duty at the American Embassy in Moscow, numerous visits to the Soviet Union, and many years in Washington with the Department of State, the United States Information Agency, the Commission on Security and Cooperation in Europe (U.S. Congress), and the National Endowment for Democracy.

When I first began to interact with Russians in the early 1960s, they had a well-earned reputation for being difficult. This was due, in part, to the Cold War mentality of the time—on both sides. But another, more fundamental factor was the inability of Americans and Russians to understand certain patterns of each other's behavior. This led me to wonder why Russians are in some ways so similar to Americans and in others so different.

Many an American has returned from a first visit to Moscow exclaiming, "I don't understand why we have had such difficulties with the Russians. They're just like us."

Subsequent visits—and a closer look—will reveal that Russians and Americans do indeed have differences. As a Russian journalist once told me, "Americans will at first see the similarities between our two peoples, but they should also look for the differences."

This book will seek to explain those differences and to help Americans understand why Russians behave like Russians. In the process some readers may also learn why they behave like Americans. There are risks, admittedly, in attempting to define national characteristics. A nation may be unfairly stereotyped, and there will always be exceptions to the rule. But who will not agree that Russians differ from Poles, Poles from Germans, and Germans from French, although these nations have lived side by side in Europe from time immemorial? And Russians in the Commonwealth are recognizably different from Armenians, Georgians (not in the Commonwealth), and Moldovans, and even more different from Azeris and Uzbeks.

The Russian character, formed over centuries by unique experiences and traditions, has made Russians different from other Europeans as well as from Americans. The characteristics described here may not apply to all Russians, but Americans can expect to see them in most of the Russians they will meet. Old traditions endure today despite the revolutions of 1917 and seventy years of communism which established a new order, and these traits will continue to influence whatever state and society evolve during the 1990s and beyond.

As French historian François Guizot has written, looking back on his own country's revolutions:

When nations have existed for a long and glorious time, they cannot break with their past, whatever they do; they are influenced by it at the very moment when they work to destroy it; in the midst of the most glaring transformations they remain fundamentally in character and destiny such as their history has formed them. Even the most daring and powerful revolutions cannot abolish national traditions of long duration. Therefore, it is most important, not only for the sake of intellectual curiosity but also for the good management of international relations, to know and to understand these traditions.[1]

---

[1]François Guizot, quoted by Hans Kohn in *The Mind of Modern Russia* (New Brunswick, NJ: Rutgers University Press, 1955), vii.

Acknowledgments

Thanks are due to David S. Hoopes, Editor-in-Chief of Intercultural Press, Inc., for conceiving the idea for this book and for his encouragement and assistance in seeing it through to completion. Judy Carl Hendrick, Assistant Editor at Intercultural Press, was most helpful with the final editing, seeing many things that I had missed.

Authors whose works I have consulted include Harley Balzer, Harold J. Berman, James H. Billington, Cyril E. Black, Robert V. Daniels, Ronald Hingley, Geoffrey Hosking, Anthony Jones, George F. Kennan, Hans Kohn, Thomas G. Masaryk, Klaus Mehnert, Wright Miller, David K. Shipler, Hedrick Smith, S. Frederick Starr, Tibor Szamuely, Dinko Tomasic, and Nicholas P. Vakar.

Former Foreign Service colleagues and friends who have reviewed portions of the manuscript or who have made helpful suggestions include Richard T. Davies, Nadia Diuk, Richard Dobson, David M. Evans, Murray Feshbach, John Finnerty, Alfred Friendly Jr., Julia Fuller, Phyllis Gestrin, David M. Goldfrank, Dina Kaminskaya, Nancy Lubin, Daniel Matuszewski, David Nalle, Robert Rand, Louise Shelley, Frantisek and Larisa Silnitsky, Konstantin Simis, Richard Stites, Johannes Van Straalen, and Irwin Weil. To Dr. Harold Orel, University of

Kansas, I am indebted for the source of the Rudyard Kipling quote on Russians.

The lectures and seminars of the Kennan Institute for Advanced Russian Studies provided the opportunity to hear many Russian and Western scholars whose views have helped me to better understand and explain Russian behavior.

The United States Information Agency (USIA) enabled me to visit Russia twice during recent years and witness the changes taking place there. In 1988, as director of a USIA book exhibit, I spent ten weeks in Moscow, Novosibirsk, Minsk, and Tbilisi, conversing with hundreds of citizens about Russia and America. And in 1989, I was in Moscow again with a USIA exhibit at the Seventh Moscow International Book Fair, talking with intellectuals and students about what Americans should know in order to better understand Russians. In quoting from some of my conversations with these members of the educated elite, I have honored their requests for anonymity. With the exception of these and other quotes, the views expressed are my own.

In transliterating Russian names and words I have made some minor changes in the usual methods in order to more closely approximate the Russian pronunciation. Where another spelling has become accepted usage in English, I have followed the more familiar form.

Yale Richmond
Washington, D.C.

Introduction

There are, at the present time, two great nations in the world which seem to tend towards the same end, although they started from different points: I allude to the Russians and the Americans. Both of them have grown up unnoticed; and whilst the attention of mankind was directed elsewhere, they have suddenly assumed a most prominent place amongst the nations; and the world learned of their existence and their greatness at almost the same time. All other nations seem to have nearly reached their natural limits, and only to be charged with the maintenance of their power; but these are still in the act of growth; all the others are stopped, or continue to advance with extreme difficulty; these are proceeding with ease and with celerity along a path to which the human eye can assign no term. The American struggles against the natural obstacles which oppose him; the adversaries of the Russian are men; the former combats the wilderness and savage life; the latter, civilization with all its weapons and its arts; the conquests of the one are therefore gained by the plough-share; those of the other by the sword. The Anglo-American relies upon personal interest to accomplish his ends, and gives free scope to the unguided exertions and common sense of the citizens; the Russian centers all the authority of society in a single arm: the principal instrument of the former is freedom; of the latter, servitude. Their *starting point is different, and their courses are not the same; yet each of them seems to be marked out by the will of Heaven to sway the destinies of half the globe.*[1]

These prescient words were written in 1835 by Alexis de Tocqueville in his epic work, *Democracy in America*. The French traveler, like many others since his time, was struck by the differences as well as the similarities between Americans and Russians.

The surface similarities are readily apparent. Russians feel a common identity with Americans as citizens of multiethnic, continental, great powers. In history both peoples have been expansionist. Americans moved west from the Atlantic coast across the Great Plains and the Rockies to the Pacific shores. Russians expanded in all directions but mostly east beyond the Ural Mountains and across the vast stretches of Siberia to the Pacific shores, and beyond to Alaska in 1741. Russians and Americans eventually met in 1812 in California, where so many new overtures seem to occur.

Both tamed a wilderness. Indeed, as Russian and American historians have noted, there is a frontier spirit shared by Siberia and the American West. The landowning gentry and the bonded serf of European Russia were not common to Siberia, which was settled by such diverse groups as Cossacks, political and religious dissidents, independent peasants, runaway serfs, and exiled convicts. Today's residents of the Siberian metropolis Novosibirsk liken it to Chicago, which they know, by reputation, as a hustling, bustling city serving a vast hinterland. And both Russians and Americans regard themselves as chosen nations with a messianic mission, destined to bring their own versions of enlightenment to less fortunate people.

America and Russia today are also nuclear powers with the capacity to destroy each other and the rest of the world as well. Likewise, they face the common challenges of reducing their awesome arsenals of armaments and of coping with the environmental consequences of their weapons industries.

Americans and Russians also think big. Both are energetic and inventive. Russians appreciate the casual, direct, and often blunt American way of speaking which they liken to their own—without pretense and much different from the West European manner which they find formal, indirect, and less sincere. Finally, Russians, despite their traditional suspicion of foreigners, show heartfelt hospitality to visitors from abroad, a trait they share with Americans.

Differences between Russians and Americans are equally apparent. Authority in America, as Tocqueville observed, has been diffused and flows upward from the people to a representative government. In Russia authority has been centralized and flows down. Pressure for change in America has come from below, and elected officials have either responded or eventually been replaced. Change in Russia has been imposed from above, and Russians have usually resisted because change there has been associated with hardship and misfortune.

In America individuals are celebrated and their rights vis-a-vis government are protected in both law and practice. In Russia, from its beginnings, individual rights have been subordinated to the greater communal good. In America pluralism and tolerance for diverse views prevail. Such diversity appears chaotic to those Russians who value consensus and a single prevailing truth. The American economy is based in the private sector and a free market, and the role of government has been minor. The Russian state, whether tsarist or communist, has distrusted the free market and has played an active role in the economy. America's cultural roots are in Western Europe. Russia's roots are in both Europe and Asia, and historians still debate which has played the greater role in shaping the Russian character.

Historical experience also separates Russians and Americans. For most of its history Russia has been in a state of almost constant warfare with neighboring nations, its people often suffering extreme cruelties and violence in their own land. Since the Civil War, America has fought its wars mostly abroad, and its people have not known wartime hardship and devastation.

Whether similar or dissimilar, America and Russia have been thrust upon the world stage in the latter half of the twentieth century as nuclear superpowers and forced, rather reluctantly, to interact with each other. Only belatedly have they discovered the many common concerns they share, the most vital of which are the preservation of peace in the nuclear age and the very survival of civilization.

These weighty concerns, however, have not led to improved understanding. Contact between Russians and Americans in the past has been limited, separated as the two peoples have been by distance, ideology, and language. Today, however, they are interacting to an extent never anticipated, and the need for improved understanding has become urgent, not merely for a few diplomats and businesspeople but for all Americans and Russians.

Examples of misunderstanding abound. After World War II the United States, unaware of the extent of the Soviet Union's devastation and losses, feared a Soviet assault on Western Europe. The Russians, in turn, regarded U.S. economic and military assistance to Western Europe as threats to their own security. Their field of vision narrowed by ideological blinders, they confidently awaited the collapse of capitalism in the West and the triumph of what they called socialism. With the onset of the Cold War, paranoia grew on both sides.

The Cuban missile crisis of 1962, which brought the two superpowers to the brink of nuclear warfare, was the most frightful example of misjudgment. More recently, *glasnost* and *perestroika* were seen by some Americans as the start of a campaign to bring democracy to the Soviet Union. Other Americans, however, saw them as public relations gambits designed to deceive the West. Clearly, the understanding gap still exists.

To help bridge that gap and to enable Americans to better understand the new Russia that is evolving, this book will focus on those forces that have shaped Russian behavior—geography, history, religion, culture, and governance—and how they differ from those that have formed American behavior.

The terms *Russian* and *Soviet* have often been used inter-changeably by both Russians and Americans (as they will be here by the author, at times). Even Soviet leaders at times have incorrectly referred to the Soviet Union as Russia although Rus-sia as a sovereign state ceased to exist in 1922 when it became the Union of Soviet Socialist Republics. And in December, 1991, reflecting the increased sovereignty of the republics and the discrediting of socialism, the Soviet Union was transformed into the Commonwealth of Independent States, a loose political alli-ance whose permanence is also questionable.

Our subject here will be the Russians rather than all of the more than one hundred nationalities that comprised the Soviet people. While Russians numbered little more than half the population, the political and economic leadership of the Soviet Union was almost entirely Russian, as well as the top echelons of the Communist party, armed forces, and KGB. Russian, more-over, was the predominant language and culture.

Whether Russian or Soviet, many changes are occurring in that distant land which Winston Churchill in 1939 described as a riddle, wrapped in a mystery, inside an enigma. Today, we know much more about Russia, but each day's news records events which no one, American or Russian, could have foreseen only a few years ago.

The nature of the changes can legitimately be questioned—are they real, what is their purpose, and how long will they last? But whatever the results of this most recent effort to modernize Russia, change there will continue to be shaped by the Russian character—and that character, formed over a millennium, has changed slowly.

Russia was communist for seventy years but has been Russian Orthodox for a thousand, and Russians have lived even longer with their harsh climate, vast expanse of forest and steppe, and geographic and cultural isolation. To understand the Russians, one must know from whence they come.

---

[1]Alexis de Tocqueville, *Democracy in America vol. 1*, translated by Henry Reeve (New York: Random House, Vintage Books, 1958), 452.

1

Welcome to Moscow

My plane to Moscow was late, arriving in the dark at Sheremetyevo Airport on a winter evening after a long flight from New York. It was not a warm welcome. The wind was bitter cold as passengers deplaned and piled aboard a bus with frosted-over windows for the short ride to the terminal. I had been traveling since the previous evening and was tired.

Inside the terminal the wait at immigration was long and tedious as young, grim-faced border guards took their time checking passports and visas. (In all my many visits to Russia, a border guard has smiled at me only once.) The customs clearance was equally long and thorough, but at last I was cleared and once more admitted to Russia.

Russian airport terminals are crowded, noisy, and chaotic as passengers mill about seeking friends and greeters. As elsewhere in the East, airport arrivals and departures bring out throngs of relatives and well-wishers, but not for me. I struggled alone with my luggage to the head of the taxi line.

After a thirty-minute drive to the city, and a hassle with the taxi driver—Russia's most zealous capitalists—who wanted to be paid in dollars, I arrived at the Ukraina. Unlike Moscow's newer hotels, the Ukraina was built in the "wedding cake" style of the Stalin era and has a musty decor that reminds a visitor of

Old Russia. I first stayed at the hotel in 1963 and over the years have become accustomed to its shabby and faded inelegance.

There was no line at the registration desk, just the usual crowd, pushing and shoving, trying to get the attention of the lone clerk. After a fifteen-minute wait, I had finally registered, given my bags to a porter, showed my hotel identification card to the ever-present guard who admitted me to the lobby, and was on my way to an upper floor. One final hassle occurred before I was settled in my room—the porter demanded to be tipped in dollars or with a pack of Marlboros (the preferred brand in Russia).

It was then that hunger hit. I had not eaten since a light lunch on my Pan American flight and was looking forward to a snack at the hotel *buffet*, a sort of Russian snack bar. But to eat at the buffet I first had to change dollars into rubles, since Soviet currency could not legally be brought into the Soviet Union.

Making my way down the long dim hall, I approached the *dyezhurnaya* (person on duty) for my floor. A feature of many Russian hotels, they are the women who keep the keys, control access to rooms, and provide hot water for tea or instant coffee (if asked politely). Inquiring about the location of the currency exchange office, I was told that it had closed for the day.

"*Shto delat*" (What to do?), I asked.

Shrugging her shoulders, she looked me over indifferently. Here was the making of a classic confrontation between a Western visitor and the Soviet system, which was not designed to serve individuals with special requests. Had I been a member of a tour group, there would have been a guide to tend to my needs, and dinner would have been planned for the group at the hotel restaurant, paid in advance, and there would have been no need to change money. But here I was, a lone American who had to get something to eat before falling into bed to catch up with the eight-hour time change from New York.

From past experience in Russia I knew not to retreat, so I stood my ground, changed the subject, and began to converse with the old lady. We talked about my long trip from the States, the purpose of my visit, the Moscow weather, where I had learned to speak Russian, the current shortages in Moscow, her children and mine, and how nice it was for me to be back in Russia again. After a while, I returned to the subject of my hunger and asked if she had any suggestions as to what I might do before the snack bar closed for the night.

"I'll lend you some rubles," she replied, reaching for her satchel under the desk, "and you can pay me back tomorrow."

My approach had worked. A kind old Russian grandmother had taken pity on a hungry American and lent him a few of her own rubles so he could get some *khleb, sir, i chai* (bread, cheese, and tea) before retiring for the night. Welcome to Moscow!

The lesson of this story—and this book—is simple. Moscow can be a cold and impersonal place, where a visitor's requests all too often meet with an automatic *nyet*. But Russians respond to a human approach, and they can be warm and helpful once a good interpersonal relationship has been established. When that point is reached, their word is good, *nyet* becomes *da*, and deals can be done. This is the key to understanding the Russians.

2

Geography and Culture

All civilizations are to some extent the product of geographical factors, but history provides no clearer example of the profound influence of geography upon a culture than in the historical development of the Russian people.

—George Vernadsky, *A History of Russia*

The Origins of Russia

One Rus has its roots in a universal, or at least in European, culture. In this Rus the ideas of goodness, honor and freedom are understood as in the West. But there is another Rus: the Rus of the dark forests, the Rus of the Taiga, the animal Russia, the fanatic Russia, the Mongol-Tatar Russia. This last Russia made despotism and fanaticism its ideal.... Kievan Rus was a part of Europe, Moscow remained the negation of Europe.

—Leo Tolstoy[1]

Mikhail Gorbachev, in 1989, endorsed the concept of a "common European home," with Russia as a tenant. In geographic terms the common European home makes sense. Europe does extend from the Atlantic Ocean to the Ural Mountains, and Russia—at least a part of it—is indeed in Europe. But through

5

much of its history, Russia has been isolated from or has rejected Europe and its Western ways. Mr. Gorbachev's common European home, with Russia occupying the back porch and the United States and Canada the front porch, is a new concept in geopolitical real estate.

The great rivers of Russia flow north and south, and along these rivers came Russia's early contacts with the outside world. From the northern rivers in the ninth century came Viking raiders and traders from Scandinavia who became the rulers of *Rus*, the city-principality of Kiev and forerunner of the Russian state. From the southern rivers came contacts with Byzantium, the Eastern half of the Christian Roman Empire and its resplendent capital, the Greek city of Constantinople (today's Istanbul), whence came Russia's religion, written language, law, and art.

Kievan Rus converted to Orthodox Christianity in 988, and Constantinople became its link to the Mediterranean and the West for commerce as well as culture. But scarcely a century later that linkage was threatened by repeated onslaughts of mounted marauders from Asia moving westward over the great Eurasian steppe. When these invaders overran the south of Russia and threatened Kiev, the Rus began to migrate north, seeking protection in remote forests inhabited at that time by Finnish tribes. Power gradually shifted from Kievan Rus to Russian Muscovy.

The Tatars, also known as Mongols, invaded Russia in the mid-thirteenth century. Unstoppable, they took Moscow in 1234 and Kiev in 1240, and made Russian princes their vassals for the next two hundred years. While the Tatar conquest did not make Asians of the Russians, it did prevent them from becoming Europeans. It also produced today's Russians—a mixture of Slavic, Finnish, and Tatar blood.

When Moscow liberated itself from the Tatar yoke in 1480, the modern Russian state was born. Distant from Europe, the new state was cut off from Constantinople which in 1453 had fallen to the Muslim Ottoman Turks. The Russian Orthodox

Church, isolated from the rest of Christianity, developed independently as a national church.

Moscow, moreover, saw itself as the Third and Last Rome, successor to Rome and Constantinople, the two capitals of the Roman Empire which in turn had fallen to barbarians and infidels. Russia was regarded by its religious and lay leaders as a holy land with an imperial mission, a new center of Christianity, destined to unite the peoples of East and West. It was at this time that Russia's rulers began to use the title *tsar*, derived from Caesar.

Russia's historic distrust of the West has its roots in this religious schism and its aftermath. Remote from the West, Russia experienced none of the major developments which shaped modern Europe—the Renaissance with its revival of classical influence and flowering of the arts, the Reformation with its pluralism of religious and secular thought, the rise of big cities, the development of modern agriculture and commerce, the scientific revolution, economic liberalism and recognition of individual rights, the beginnings of political liberty, and the growth of a strong middle class. In the West the middle class was in the forefront of reform. Russia's failure to develop a strong middle class delayed reform.

Cut off from the West, Russia remained a vast, backward, largely agricultural empire, regimented and ruled by an autocratic dynasty with a holy mission to defend its faith against the barbarians of the East and the heresies and pluralism of the West.

The pluralism of the West, moreover, was seen by Russia as chaotic, a cacophony of voices without harmony, a disunity of thought and purpose. To this West, nevertheless, Russia would come during its periodic attempts to modernize—seeking science, technology, and administrative know-how—but rejecting at the same time the Western thought that came with the modernization it so sorely needed.

To remote Russia and its Soviet successor state, many things Western have come late—manufacturing, higher education, science and technology, the management sciences, and computers as well as blue jeans and rock music. Other things Western have not yet arrived—good government, democracy, and efficiency. These come from a West that Russia has openly disdained but secretly envied and from which it is today again trying to learn.

The Cold North

The aim of civilization in the North is serious. There, society is the fruit, not of human pleasures, not of interests and passions easily satisfied, but of a will ever persisting and ever thwarted which urges the people to incomprehensible efforts. There, if individuals unite together, it is to struggle with a rebellious nature, which unwillingly responds to the demands made upon her.

—Custine, *Empire of the Czar*

Mention the Russian winter and most Americans will think of deep snow, piled to the rooftops. Actually, the snow is not that deep and winter is known more for its frigid temperatures, which Russians find invigorating. Those temperatures, however, can become unbearable when the wind blows across the open land and the windchill factor plummets.

Russia is a northern country. Moscow lies on the same latitude as the lower Hudson Bay. Russia's northernmost port, Murmansk, is further north than Nome, Alaska. The southern port, Odessa (in Ukraine), is further north than Minneapolis.

Nature has not been kind to Russia. Much of European Russia and Siberia is very cold most of the year, like Canada and our northern Plains states. Autumn is brief and followed by a long and severe winter. Summers are short and hot. In Old Russia, where the economy was mostly agricultural, peasants could do little during winter months and they more or less hibernated, holed up in their huts, seeking to survive while awaiting spring and the sowing season.

When spring did arrive, there was much to be done, and in a short span of time. In Russia's northern lands there is less than five months from spring, when the ground can be tilled and seed planted, until fall, when crops must be harvested before the first frost. During these precious few months, Russians over the centuries have worked almost around the clock to produce the food needed to get them through the following winter. According to one popular theory, this explains why Russians often appear inactive for long periods of time and then show intense bursts of energy. The stagnation of the Brezhnev era, for example, can be seen as a long winter of hibernation, and the perestroika of the Gorbachev years as a short spring and summer of frenzied effort.

The harsh climate explains the Russians' strength, their ability to endure extreme hardship, and their bleak outlook on life as well as their patience and submission. Climate has also made them cautious. In Russia's farmlands weather is often unpredictable and crop failure an ever-present possibility. In an agricultural society where survival depends on the weather, it is imprudent to take chances. And, as in all traditional societies, the test of time is preferred to the risks of the new and untried.

Does climate still make a difference in the final years of the twentieth century? Over millennia, people everywhere have adapted to their environment, and today some have even tamed it. Americans, with their central heating, air conditioning, and other modern conveniences, have literally insulated themselves from weather's extremes. American culture and character today are not much different in Minnesota from states with milder climes.

Russians, however, have been living in their cold north for centuries and, for much of that time, as peasants and serfs in a primitive agricultural society. In contrast to Americans, most Russians have lived, until recently, much as their ancestors did before them—in small villages, distant and isolated, their freedom of movement restricted, and without the comforts and labor-saving tools provided by modern society. The cold north is still very much in their bones.

Distance and Isolation

> Forced to withdraw into the northeastern corner of Europe and to use all their strength there in the difficult labor of national unification, the Russian people found themselves, from the thirteenth century on, physically separated from the rest of the Christian world.
>
> —S. M. Solovyov, *Peter's Reforms*

Most countries have only one time zone. The United States has four, and Americans in the East who watch a football game in California know that there is a three-hour time difference. Russia, however, has eleven time zones and is more than twice the size of the United States, stretching six thousand miles from St. Petersburg in the west to the Bering Straits in the east. A trip from Moscow to the Pacific via the famous Trans-Siberian Railway takes seven days.

This vast landmass—one-seventh of the earth's surface—has only limited access to the sea. Deep in its Eurasian remoteness, Russia has been distant from Europe, the Mediterranean, the Middle East, China, and other great centers of civilization. Moscow is some three thousand miles from Paris, and before the age of the railroad such an arduous journey could take more than a month.

The two momentous events mentioned in an earlier section—the Tatar (Mongol) invasion of the thirteenth century which cut Russia off from Europe for 250 years and the fall of Constantinople (the center of Eastern Christianity) to the Turks in 1453—caused Russia's commercial, cultural, and religious isolation and retarded its development for centuries, a handicap from which it has never fully recovered.

Distance and isolation also deterred development of a mercantile tradition. Self-sufficient in agriculture and natural resources, and with no great need to trade with other countries, Russia became inwardly oriented. Contacts with the outside world were through neighboring states, and when conflicts arose with those states, they were often resolved by military force, ending with the absorption of new lands.

Geography also made Russia vulnerable to wars—literally hundreds of them—along her lengthy borders which have no natural defenses. To the east, the great Eurasian steppe served as a highway for waves of invaders from Asia who, in ancient times, repeatedly swept into Russia. From the west, Russia has been invaded by Teutonic Knights, Lithuanians, Poles, Swedes, French, and Germans. And to the south, Russia has had continuous wars over the centuries with Turkic peoples.

As a result of this constant border warfare, Russia became the largest state (actually an empire) on earth. Its expansion, moreover, resulted in even longer undefined borders as well as heightened suspicion of neighboring nations.

With such a vast territory to govern, Russia evolved into a state ruled from its center and organized along paramilitary lines. Service to the state was a duty for both nobles and peasants. Surrounded by hostile powers, Russia became dependent on the use of force in its relations with neighboring states and obsessed with security—traits that still survive. Although the Tatars invaded Russia some seven hundred years ago, the memory of their harsh rule is one reason for Russia's deep-rooted suspicion of China today. But with more than one billion Chinese on the other side of an indefensible and oft-contested border 4,200 miles long, this fear is perhaps understandable.

How has a state ringed by so many adversaries been able to continually extend its territorial reach? As Russians see it, they have been victims of foreign aggression, and Russia's expansion beyond her natural borders is a consequence of victories over foreign invaders. As others see it, Russia has taken advantage of weakness or instability in neighboring states to annex territories along her periphery.

One sharp critic of Russian territorial aggrandizement in the midnineteenth century was a London-based correspondent of the *New York Tribune* named Karl Marx. In 1852, in his coverage of events leading to the Crimean War, Marx wrote:

> Russia's acquisitions from Sweden are greater than what remains of that kingdom; from Poland, nearly equal to the Austrian empire; from Turkey in Europe, greater than Prussia (exclusive of the Rhenish provinces); from Turkey in Asia, as large as the whole dominion of Germany proper; from Persia, equal to England; from Tartary, to an extent as large as European Turkey, Greece, Italy, and Spain, taken together. The total acquisitions of Russia during the last sixty years are equal in extent and importance to the whole Empire she had in Europe before that time.[2]

Along with her territorial expansion, Russia has sought protection from excessive foreign influence. Periodic attempts to introduce European technology and Western ways were accepted by the small ruling class, but these efforts at modernization met with the sullen resistance of the Russian people. Suspicion and mistrust of foreigners—the West in particular—has been a recurring theme in both Russian and Soviet history, and the Iron Curtain of the Soviet era is its most recent manifestation. New ideas have come late to Russia, when they have come at all.

The United States has also been expansionist and a continental power, but with a maritime and commercial tradition. The Atlantic and Pacific oceans served as natural defenses, providing protection from foreign aggression and ensuring the peace necessary for economic development at home and trade abroad. The American fixation with freedom of the seas can be compared with Russia's obsession with security along her borders. The objective of both countries has been to ensure stability and well-being at home.

America's commercial experience and Russia's lack of a mercantile tradition have given the two countries different world outlooks. As Richard Pipes points out: "Commerce is...by its very nature conducive to compromise. Nations raised on it instinctively seek a common ground for agreement, that exact point at which the other side might be prepared to make a deal."[3] Compromise is native to America but not to Russia. The oceans, moreover, have been bridges for America, providing easy access to other countries and cultures. New ideas have usually been welcomed, or at least not opposed; and the oceans served as highways for waves of immigrants who came in peace and with hope, turning their backs on the rigid class divisions of the Old World to seek a better life in the New. They brought vitality and new talent to a constantly changing and dynamic society.

The New World is indeed new, only some four hundred years old, compared to Russia's more than one thousand. Russians, moreover, have been living in their native environment from time immemorial, and change has come slowly. The new has been welcomed in America, the old has been revered in Russia.

Communalism

> Together in the mir we will move even mountains.
>
> —Russian proverb

The Moscow home of Fyodor Chaliapin, the world-renowned Russian basso, is located next to the American Embassy on Novinsky Boulevard. It is a fine example of how prominent Moscow residents lived in Old Russia. The building was closed, however, during my years at the embassy and subsequent visits to the Soviet Union.

Arriving in Moscow in 1989, I learned that the Chaliapin home had been opened to the public, and I looked forward to a visit. A colleague inquired about visiting hours and was told that the museum was open to groups but not to individuals. Unfazed, we rounded up some friends and, as members of a group, spent a delightful hour in Old Russia. When in Moscow, do as the Muscovites do.

The affinity for the group has deep roots in Russian culture and can still be seen today in everyday life. In boy-girl relationships, for example, if an American asks a Russian girl for a date and she accepts, he will be surprised when several other Russians accompany them. This should not be seen as reflecting distrust of a foreigner and his intentions but rather as a preference for the group over the individual.

Russians carry their group ethic with them. An American friend in Washington relates how he often calls one of his emigré friends and suggests that they go to a movie. "Fine," says the Russian, "but let me call some friends and see if they would like to go with us." This turns off the American who does not like to go to movies in groups.

Sobornost (communal spirit, togetherness) distinguishes Russians from Westerners for whom individualism and competitiveness are more common characteristics. As Nicolas Zernov puts it, in Russia there is the desire "...to find the balance between the conflicting outlooks of Europe and Asia, between Western claims to personal freedom and Oriental insistence on the integration of the individual into the community."[4]

In a society where the communal good takes priority over individual needs and rights, mutual dependence is a unifying factor. Russian communalism is not an invention of Communists, although its traditions were exploited under the Soviets. Its origins lie deep in the vastness of the great Russian Plain.

In prehistoric times Russians banded together to fell the forest, till the soil, harvest the crops, and protect themselves from invaders and marauders. Tools and weapons were primitive and life was harsh, but these handicaps could be overcome and survival ensured—although just barely—by the collective effort of living and working together.

The *zadruga*, a clan or greater family commune, served as the nucleus of a tribal society. In time, it evolved into a larger unit, the *mir*, an agricultural village commune (also known as *obshchina*) based on territory and mutual interests. Member families lived in small hamlets, in huts side by side. The surrounding land was held in common by the mir, and was unfenced. Each family, however, had its own hut, maintained a small plot of land for a family garden, and took its meals at home. Land utilization was the mir's primary purpose and the basis for its survival. The mir determined how much of the common land each family would work, depending on its size and needs. It decided which crops would be grown and when they would be planted and harvested. It collected taxes and settled local disputes. Its authority, moreover, extended beyond land matters. It also disciplined members, intervened in family disputes, settled issues which affected the community as a whole, and otherwise regulated the affairs of its self-contained and isolated agricultural world.

Mir, in fact, has three meanings—village commune, world, and peace—and for its members it symbolized all three. This little world of the Russian peasant—the bulk of the populace—was a world apart from, and at least a century behind, the lifestyles of landowners and city dwellers.

Decisions of the mir were made in a village assembly of heads of households. All members could speak and discussions were lively, but no vote was taken. The objective was to determine the collective will, and after an issue had been thoroughly discussed and opposition to it had ceased, a consensus evolved which became binding on all households. Richard Stites describes the mir meetings as marked by "...seemingly immense disorder and chaos, interruptions, and shouting; in fact it achieved business-like results."[5]

When peasants moved to cities as workers and craftsmen, they brought with them their communal way of life and formed workers' cooperatives, called *artels*. Modeled on the mir, artel members hired themselves out for jobs as a group and shared the payments for their work. Stites describes how some artels rented communal apartments where they would share the rent, buy the food, dine together, and even attend leisure events as a group. Hundreds of thousands of workers lived in this way in the generation or so before the Revolution.[6] In the city, as in the village, security and survival were ensured by a collective effort.

This communal way of life persisted well into the twentieth century, lasting longer in Russia than elsewhere in Europe. Tsarist Russia encouraged the mir because it served as a form of state control over the peasants, facilitating tax collection and military conscription. Because the mir affected so many people, it played a major role in forming the Russian character.

As Lev Tikhomirov—appropriately, with a *mir* in the middle of his name—wrote in 1888: "The Great Russian cannot imagine a life outside his society, outside the mir...The Great Russian says: 'The mir is a fine fellow, I will not desert the mir. Even death is beautiful in common."[7]

Serfdom (personal bondage) was imposed on most Russian peasants in the late sixteenth century and lasted for three hundred years before being abolished in 1861 (two years before slavery ended in America). The emancipation of serfs was accompanied by a land redistribution that enabled freed serfs, in principle, to purchase land outside the commune. However, land distributed under the reform was actually given to the mir, which held it in common until its members could make redemption payments.

This freed the serfs but preserved the mir, and peasants once more found themselves tied to the land they worked, since most of them were financially unable to leave the commune. The reform thus continued the mir's power over peasants and their submission to a higher authority which regulated the social order.

Service to the state also continued. The emancipation was accompanied by a reduction in the length of obligatory military service for former serfs and the lower class of townspeople. After 1861, the length of duty for those selected was reduced from twenty-five to sixteen years! A later reform, in 1874, made military service compulsory for all able-bodied males over age twenty; the normal tour of active duty was further reduced to six years but was followed by nine years in the reserve and five more in the militia.

The mir endured in various forms until 1930, when it was replaced by yet another form of communal life, the Soviet collective farm. A modern-day effort by the state to tie peasants to the land, the brutally enforced collectivization was strongly opposed by the peasants. The objective was to ensure an adequate supply of food for the cities, which were to grow under the industrialization of the Five-Year Plans. The immediate result, however, was famine and the death of millions in the countryside.

The contrast between Russian communalism and American individualism can best be seen in the differences between Russian peasants and American farmers. America's agricultural settlers were independent farmers and ranchers who owned their land and lived on it, self-sufficient and distant from their neighbors. In contrast to peasants of the mir, America's farmers lived behind fences which marked the limits of their property. The Americans, moreover, were entrepreneurs in the sense that they managed their holdings individually, taking economic risks and regulating their own affairs, independent of the state.

America also had its communes—and still has some today—an indication of some innate urge to band and bond together. America's communes, however, have existed on the fringes of society rather than at its center. In America the commune is considered alien, in Russia it is native.

Individualism is esteemed in America, but in Russian the word has a pejorative meaning. Steeped in the heritage of the mir, Russians think of themselves as members of a community rather than as individuals. The communal spirit helps to explain many of their characteristics—behavior in crowds, for example.

Physical contact with complete strangers—anathema to Americans—does not bother Russians. In crowds, they touch, push, shove, and even use elbows without hard feelings—except in the ribs of those who are competing with them to obtain access to something. Americans should not take such pokes personally. Politeness takes different forms in different societies, and behavior in crowds may vary.

A crowd of passengers attempting to board a ship in Odessa in the early 1960s caught the attention of British traveler Laurens van der Post. A ship's officer stood on the quay collecting tickets at the gangway. The crowd pushed and jostled but never lost its temper. Although it shouted at the officer and elbowed him out of the way, he did not appear irritated, nor did he attempt to call them to order. A Russian friend related to van der Post how a group of French tourists, caught earlier in the same situation and annoyed by the crowd's persistent jostling, had lost their tempers and lashed out angrily at everyone near them. "The Russians were horrified at such lack of traveling manners," writes van der Post, "presumably because it was personal retaliation and not the collective, impersonal pressure they were all applying to get through a bottleneck."[8]

Accustomed to close physical contact, Russian men, as well as women, hold hands while strolling the streets and touch when talking. Women dance with other women if there are not enough men to go around or if not asked by a man for a dance. Russian men embrace and kiss each other, on lips as well as cheeks, as I learned once when I had a male kiss planted on my lips, much to my surprise, at the end of a long and festive evening. Americans are advised, however, not to initiate such spontaneous displays of affection, as President Jimmy Carter learned when he kissed Leonid Brezhnev (on the cheek) at their Vienna summit, much to Brezhnev's surprise and embarrassment.

On entering a restaurant, Russians will not hesitate to join strangers rather than dine alone at an empty table as Americans would prefer. In Russian restaurants, one seldom sees diners seated at tables in ones or twos; more likely they will be seated in large groups of as many as twenty persons. Russians will not be offended by Americans joining them at their tables and will welcome the opportunity to converse with their new dinner companions. Many of the most insightful conversations occur when Russians and Americans find themselves seated side by side in restaurants, railroad compartments, and airplanes.

Recreational activities are often arranged in groups, as in the artel. After working together all day, factory and office employees will spend evenings in group excursions to theaters and other cultural events organized by their shop stewards. Indeed, tickets to such events are more easily obtained by members of a group rather than by individuals. And what foreign visitor to Russia has not fumed when large tourist groups were given priority service by waiters in hotel dining rooms while individual tourists were left to wait at their tables.

American students at Russian universities are expected to act as a group and elect a *starosta* (elder or senior person) to speak for them in their relations with the university administration. One American starosta recalls how the student council decided to organize a basketball league and asked the Americans if they wanted to play. Sure, said the American starosta, but he suggested that Americans would prefer to play intramurals—show up, form a pickup team, shoot a few baskets, and get some exercise. This was unacceptable to the student council which wanted organized national teams to compete. Accordingly, the Americans began to recruit players but, finding only two who wanted to play, had to add an Austrian, Hungarian, and Bulgarian to round out their team (which was roundly trounced).

Russians seem compelled to intrude into the private affairs of others. Older Russians admonish young men and women—complete strangers—for perceived wrongdoings, using the impersonal term of address, *molodoy chelovek* (young man) or *dyevushka* (girl). On the street, older women volunteer advice to young mothers on the care of their children. American parents in Moscow have been accosted by Russian women and accused of not dressing their children properly for the severe winter. One American, whose child was clad in well-insulated outerwear, would respond by unzipping her child's jacket and inviting the Russian women to feel how warm her child's body actually was. In a collective society, everybody's business is also everyone else's. (One intrusion that is appreciated—and expected—is to inform others when they show the telltale white skin blotches that indicate the onset of frostbite.)

Russians do not hesitate to visit a friend's home without advance notice, even dropping in unexpectedly late at night as long as a light can be seen in a window. They routinely offer overnight accommodations to friends who are visiting their cities, a gesture based not only on their tradition of hospitality to travelers but also on today's shortage of decent overnight hotel accommodations. Americans who are accepted as friends by Russians will find that they too may receive unexpected visits by their new friends.

Marital infidelity, a private and personal matter in the West, can become a communal affair in Russia. When a husband cheats on his wife, she will often report the offense to her husband's work supervisor who—as in the mir—will call in the offender for a rebuke and lecture. Communist party members have been publicly berated at Party meetings for marital indiscretions. And in a recent Russian film, "Lonely Woman Seeks Life Companion," the lonely woman is lectured by her work supervisor who does not approve of the man who has answered her "in search of" ad.

Communism reinforced the Russian communal ethic but also added a coercive element, as illustrated by an *anekdot* (humorous story) about a schoolteacher who was lecturing her class on the virtues of *kollektivnost* (collective spirit).

"What did you do today, Ivan, to help your fellow citizens?" she asked.

"I helped an old lady to cross the street," replied Ivan.

"Very good," said the teacher who turned to Boris and asked what he had done.

"I helped Ivan to help the old lady cross the street," answered Boris.

"Excellent," said the teacher, lauding their joint effort. "And Mikhail," she continued, "what did you do?"

"I helped Boris to help Ivan to help the old lady cross the street," said Mikhail.

"Splendid," exclaimed the teacher, pleased by their kollektivnost. "But why," she asked, "did it take three strong young boys to help one old lady to cross the street?"

"She didn't want to cross," replied the boys.

Nationality

> Throughout Russian history one dominating theme has been the frontier; the theme of the struggle of the mastering of the resources of an untamed country, expanded into a continent by the ever-shifting movement of the Russian people and their conquest of and intermingling with other peoples.
> —B. H. Sumner, *A Short History of Russia*

No greater mistake can be made by a visitor to the former Soviet Union than to assume that every Russian-speaking person encountered will be a Russian. Russia is a multinational state comprising people of different nations.

The difference is nationality—the "nation" or ethnic group that an individual belongs to, and often the religion adhered to. The Russians are only one—albeit the largest—of more than a hundred nationalities in that vast land, each with its own culture and language or dialect. In the 1990s, the nationality question looms large. National consciousness is on the rise, and people who interact with Russians and other ethnic groups should appreciate its significance.

Russia's territorial expansion began in the sixteenth century, and over the next three hundred years it continually annexed along its periphery—north, south, east, and west—lands with non-Russian nationalities. How to deal with these nationalities in a vast empire ruled from its Russian center was a concern of both Russian tsars and Soviet commissars.

With a population of 290 million in 1990, the Soviet Union was the world's third most populous country—after China and India. A little more than 50 percent were Great Russians, so-called to distinguish them from their close cousins, Ukrainians

(18 percent) and Belarusians (3.6 percent) who share a common Christian heritage and speak related Slavic languages. Other major nationalities with a Christian heritage were Georgians and Armenians (3 percent); Lithuanians, Latvians, and Estonians in the Baltic republics (3 percent); and Moldovans (1 percent). The three Baltic republics were recognized as independent by Moscow in September, 1991, and other republics followed their lead in December when the Soviet Union ceased to exist and was replaced by the Commonwealth of Independent States.

In the nations with a Christian heritage, nationality and religion are interrelated. Great Russians and Belarusians are Russian Orthodox. Ukrainians may be Ukrainian Autocephalous Orthodox or, in the Western Ukraine which for centuries was a part of Poland, Ukrainian Catholic (Uniate), a church that uses the Eastern rite but is in union with the Roman Catholic Church in recognizing the authority of the Pope of Rome. Lithuanians are Roman Catholic by virtue of having been part of the Polish-Lithuanian Commonwealth for four centuries. Latvians and Estonians are Lutheran, a heritage of their German colonization and Swedish rule. Armenians and Georgians, who have their own churches, have been Christian since A.D. 301 and A.D. 318 respectively. Moldovans, like their fellow Romanians, are Orthodox.

Nations with an Islamic or Turkic heritage constituted another 20 percent of the population, the major nationalities being Azeris, Kazakhs, Kyrgyz, Tajiks, Tatars, Turkmen, and Uzbeks. And in the far north live many Arctic peoples with distinct cultures similar to those of their North American cousins.

The three Slavic nations—Russians, Ukrainians, and Belarusians—made up about 70 percent of the total Soviet population. Ukrainians and Belarusians differ somewhat from Russians. Belarus and the Western Ukraine, as noted above, were under Polish rule from the fourteenth to the eighteenth centuries, and western portions of these lands again belonged to Poland between the two World Wars. As a result, many Ukrainians and Belarusians appear more Western than do Russians. Ukraine, moreover, is located in a southern, more temperate zone and was the breadbasket of the Soviet Union. As "southerners," Ukrainians tend to be more outgoing and optimistic than their northern cousins. Throughout much of modern history the Great Russians have been a bare majority in their own country. Today, a declining Russian birthrate and an Islamic birthrate two to three times that of the Slavic and other European groups are a cause of concern to Moscow. By the year 2000 the Russian portion of the population is expected to fall below 50 percent, giving Russians less than a plurality in the Commonwealth. (A similar phenomenon is being experienced in the United States, where Americans of European origin are expected to number less than 50 percent by the middle of the next century.)

The major nationalities live in newly sovereign republics or so-called autonomous regions. In these areas, national languages and cultures have survived despite attempts at Russification, but local politics were controlled, until recently, by the Moscow center.

To further complicate this ethnic mosaic, some sixty-five million citizens live outside their republics or places of origin. Among them, in addition to twenty-five million Russians, are Germans, Jews, Poles, and others without their own designated territories. (In the 1920s, reacting to the challenge of Zionism, the Soviet Union established a Jewish Autonomous Region around Birobijan on the China border. Birobijan, however, has never attracted many Jews, and its population today is largely Russian.)

While the major nationalities now have their own local governments, languages, and cultures, the Russians were the ruling nationality of the Soviet Union, and the study of Russian was compulsory in all schools. Interest in native languages has increased in recent years, but Russian is still the lingua franca of the Commonwealth. Moreover, what was known as the Soviet Union, which was founded in 1922, was previously called Russia.

For these reasons, the terms Russian and Soviet were often used interchangeably, although not always correctly. The agglomeration of various republics and autonomous regions that have chosen to join constitute the Commonwealth. Russia today is actually the Russian Federation, a vast area extending from St. Petersburg (formerly Leningrad) to the Pacific Ocean, comprising three-fourths of the former Soviet Union territory, and with a little more than half its population and most of its natural resources. (In June 1991, voters of Leningrad elected to restore the old name of their city, St. Petersburg, and the change was approved by the Russian Parliament in September.)

Americans also live in a multinational or multicultural state that has one dominant language and one dominant culture, "Anglo." Americans, therefore, may find it difficult to comprehend the complexity of Russia's nationality problems and to appreciate their political importance.

The difference lies in two almost contradictory aspects of American culture. One is America's role as a melting pot during its first 175 years of nationhood, absorbing waves of immigrants from many parts of Europe who in time were assimilated to the dominant American culture. Within a few generations the old-world languages of the immigrants were largely lost, and cultural ties to the old country became mostly a matter of sentiment. Americans, however, also recognize that theirs is a pluralistic society composed of different backgrounds and races, and they pride themselves on their ability to create unity in diversity— although doing so with new ethnic groups is proving more difficult than during the melting pot era.

In Russia ethnic diversity is a completely different phenomenon, based on centuries of residence by the various nationalities in their historic regions of origin and on their determination to preserve their distinct languages and cultures. Nationality, moreover, is officially recognized by the government and is stated in each citizen's identification document.

In Western and Central Europe nationality as a political issue was largely resolved during the late nineteenth and early twentieth centuries. To be sure, the formation of new nation states and the redrawing of borders, particularly after World War I, did not impose perfect solutions. Nationality problems still exist today in Belgium, Bulgaria, Czechoslovakia, Finland, Italy, Romania, Spain, and Yugoslavia. But nationality issues do not threaten the existence of these states, Yugoslavia and Czechoslovakia excepted.

In the East, however, nationalism and ethnicity have reemerged in the 1990s as divisive forces which caused the breakup of the Soviet Union. All fifteen republics, including the Russian, had by 1991 proclaimed their independence or sovereignty. Centuries-old ethnic and national rivalries and passions caused outbreaks of violence between non-Russian nationalities—Azeris and Armenians, Uzbeks and Mshkets, Georgians and Ossetians—as well as between Russians and non-Russians. Attempts by Moscow at Russification, as Soviet authorities learned, are resisted in our time as strongly as they were under the tsars.

In reaction to these ethnic stirrings, there has been a revival of traditional Russian moral and spiritual values and a renewed interest in Russian Orthodoxy. Russian nationalism is also on the rise. Fearful of the demands of other nationalities, many Russians regret the breakup of the Soviet Union and the threat to its status as a great power.

In Old Russia, nationality was always an issue to be considered in political life. Today, with the threat it poses for the future of Russia, the issue has become critical. Citizens are very much aware of their nationality. Proud of their ethnicity, they are also curious about the nationality of persons they encounter. They will be pleased to tell Americans about their own nationality, and Americans should not hesitate to ask.

Russian Orthodoxy

A man who was not Orthodox could not be Russian.
—Dostoyevsky, *The Possessed*

Russian ethnicity, culture, and nationalism are identified with

Russian Orthodoxy, the state religion of Russia for almost a thousand years. In every ethnic Russian there is an Orthodox heritage. It can emerge when least expected, even among convinced Communists.

The spirit of Lenin, the founding father of the Soviet state, was regarded by orthodox Communists as immortal, as embodied in the popular slogan, "Lenin lived, Lenin lives, Lenin will live." And to remind Muscovites of Lenin's immortality, in 1969 during the celebration of the anniversary of his birth, which fell at Easter time, an image of Lenin was projected at night by searchlight onto a large balloon in the skies high above the Kremlin. The significance was not lost on Russians who address each other at Easter with the traditional Orthodox greeting, "Christ is risen."

Easter, the principal Russian religious holiday, has a special meaning for Russians. As Zernov explains, Easter signifies the resurrection of nature when, after six months of the immobility and death of winter, life suddenly returns to the land. Historically, the end of two centuries of Mongol rule is seen as a resurrection of the Russian people, achieved through their Christian faith. But at Easter, the Resurrection has its full meaning for Russians in Christ's victory over sin and death. "The service on Easter night," writes Zernov, "is an experience which has no parallel in the worship of other nations. Only those who have been present at this service can realize all that the Resurrection means to the Russian people."[9]

The origins of the Russian Church are in Byzantium, the Eastern branch of Christianity. Through its Byzantine beginnings the Russian Church regards itself as a direct descendant of the early Christian communities. From Byzantium also came the belief that Orthodox Christianity, as James Billington puts it,

had solved all the basic problems of belief and worship. All that was needed was "right praising" (the literal translation of *pravoslavie*, the Russian version of the Greek *orthodoxos*) through forms of worship handed down by the Apostolic Church and defined for all time by its seven ecumenical councils. Changes in dogma or even sacred phraseology could not be tolerated, for there was but one answer to any controversy.[10]

The consensus of the Orthodox congregation was seen as the truth—a singularity of truth in which there was no room for a pluralism of opinion. In this idea lie the roots of Russia's traditional disdain for dissidents—political as well as religious. The Russian word for dissidents, *inakomyslyaschi*, actually means persons who think differently.

The Russian sense of community and egalitarianism also has roots in Orthodoxy. *Sobor*, the Russian word for cathedral (as well as council), indicates a coming together of congregants who share common Christian values. Stites describes sobor as signifying a "sense of harmonious spiritual community."[11]

The word is symbolic to Russians who have regarded Catholicism as too authoritarian and Protestantism as too individualistic. Catholicism was traditionally seen as authoritarian because each Catholic and each national church must submit to the authority of the Pope. Protestantism was too individualistic because each national church could make its own religious doctrine and could be further splintered from within. In Orthodoxy, by contrast, as Paul Miliukov put it, "A national authority could never conflict with the universal doctrine of the Eastern church, because the national churches had no power to introduce changes into the universal doctrine, and the universal doctrine had not been invested with power."[12]

Thus, while churches in the West labored vigorously to achieve independence in religious matters, in the East the creation of national churches came easily because there was no need to question religious doctrine which, as Billington noted above, had been defined for all time and was universally accepted. Russia was the first state to have a national Orthodox church, but its example was followed later by Greece, Georgia, Serbia, Romania, Bulgaria, and others. While autonomous, they are all members of the one Eastern church.

Russian Orthodoxy is also seen as egalitarian, a fellowship uniting all souls under a single and correct religious rite. The Orthodox vision of sobornost is described by Zernov as "the main driving force behind all the social and political endeavors of the Russian...the expression of the desire to treat their rapidly expanding state as one big family."[13]

Under the Soviets, atheism became official doctrine, and the Orthodox Church, with its tradition of submission to state authority—another legacy of Byzantium—proved easy to suppress and vulnerable to Communist control. From a historical perspective, in Old Russia there was one church, one truth, and little tolerance for dissidents. In the Soviet era—at least before 1985—the Communist party replaced the Church, and Party ideology supplanted religious truth, while intolerance of dissidents greatly increased and became state policy.

Since 1985 the severe antireligious policies of the Stalin years have been reversed. A law on religious freedom was passed in 1990, and militant atheism was dropped from the Party platform in 1991. Russians today, Communists included, are showing renewed interest in their Church, responding to a rebirth of interest in Russian cultural traditions as well as a revival of concern for moral values. Two public opinion polls conducted in 1990 concluded that there were close to ninety million believers of different denominations in the Soviet Union, a figure likely to be revised upward when more complete data become available.[14]

In the 1990s the old distinctions between Eastern and Western Christianity are not so important to the average believer as they were in the past, and there is a greater receptivity to some form of ecumenism. Indeed, many Russians welcomed the election of the Polish Pope John Paul II, taking pride in him as a fellow Slav.

Churches have reopened and religious institutions are now free to do charitable work. In 1991 Orthodox Christmas (which falls in January under the old Julian calendar) was proclaimed a state holiday in the Russian, Ukrainian, and Moldovan republics for the first time since 1918. Religious worship has been resumed in a cathedral in the Moscow Kremlin. Mass is celebrated on Easter Sunday in St. Basil's, the magnificent, brilliantly colored onion-dome cathedral on Moscow's Red Square. Boris Yeltsin has attended the Easter midnight service at Moscow's Cathedral of the Epiphany. And Mr. Gorbachev, although a nonbeliever, has admitted publicly that his mother is a believer and that he himself was baptized as a child, adding that he thought this "quite normal."[15] Clearly, Orthodoxy is still a force in Russia.

The most popular book at the 1989 Moscow International Book Fair was a Russian-language edition of the Bible, which most Russian believers had never seen. Unpublished for many years, the Bible had been available only on the black market, and at prohibitive prices. Visitors to the Book Fair lined up daily, waiting patiently for free copies, ten thousand of which were distributed by an American Christian publishing house. The line of Christians waiting each day for Bibles was matched only by the throng of Russian Jews trying to gain access to the Hebrew and Jewish books exhibited by American Jewish publishers.

America, by contrast, has had neither a state church, an official ideology, nor a single truth. Rather, America has known a pluralism of beliefs and truths and has tolerated, if not encouraged, dissenters from these truths. Church and state have been kept separate, religion and ideology have been excluded from state affairs, and diverse views have been welcomed. Indeed, the very right to be different has been respected. America was settled initially by large numbers of religious and political dissidents from Europe who were more interested in worshiping God in their own way than in imposing their beliefs on others outside their religious communities.

Universal systems of thought have been resisted by Americans, as well as ideologies which purport to have the answers to all questions and a grand plan for future action. If Americans do have an ideology, it is pragmatism—if it works, do it. In Russia, creating a consensus, whether in religion or politics, has been seen as desirable, and dissidents somewhat strange—if not at times insane—for refusing to join it. According to Harvard's Edward Keenan, Russians have a tendency to embrace a philosophical system which is not theirs to begin with, and after time to proclaim themselves the sole custodians of its true interpretation.[16]

---

[1]Leo Tolstoy, quoted by Bertram D. Wolfe in *Three Who Made a Revolution* (Boston: Beacon Press, 1955), 18.

[2]Karl Marx, quoted by Paul B. Henze in "Marx on Russians and Muslims," *Central Asian Survey* 6, no. 4 (1987): 36.

[3]Richard Pipes, *U.S.-Soviet Relations in the Era of Detente* (Boulder: Westview Press, 1981), 16.

[4]Nicolas Zernov, *The Russians and Their Church* (Crestwood, NY: St. Vladimir's Seminary Press, 1978), 176.

[5]Richard Stites, *Revolutionary Dreams, Utopian Vision and Experimental Life in the Russian Revolution* (New York: Oxford University Press, 1989), 124.

[6]Ibid., 207.

[7]Lev A. Tikhomirov, *Russia, Political and Social*, quoted by Wright Miller in *Russians as People* (New York: E. P. Dutton and Company, 1961), 81.

[8]Laurens van der Post, *Journey into Russia* (Harmondsworth, England: Penguin Books, 1965), 173.

[9]Zernov, *Russians and Their Church*, 179.

[10]James H. Billington, *The Icon and the Axe, An Interpretive History of Russian Culture* (New York: Random House, Vintage Books, 1970), 6.

[11]Stites, *Revolutionary Dreams*, 16.

[12]Paul Miliukov, *Outline of Russian Culture, Part I, Religion and the Church*, edited by Michael Karpovich (New York: A. S. Barnes, 1960), 134.

[13]Zernov, *Russians and Their Church*, 182.

[14]Oxana Antic, "Statistics on Religion Speak a Language of Their Own," *Report on the USSR* 3, no. 2 (11 January 1991): 9.

[15]*Washington Post*, 6 July 1989.

[16]Edward L. Keenan, in a lecture at the Kennan Institute, Washington, D.C., 24 September 1985, and in an interview with the author, 22 March 1991.

Culture and Character

The Russian is a delightful person till he tucks in his shirt. As an oriental he is charming. It is only when he insists upon being treated as the most easterly of western peoples instead of the most westerly of easterns that he becomes a racial anomaly and extremely difficult to handle. The host never knows which side of his nature is going to turn up next.
— Rudyard Kipling, *The Man Who Was*

Egalitarianism

The interests of distribution and egalitarianism always predominated over those of production and creativity in the minds and emotions of the Russian intelligentsia.
— Nikolai Berdyaev, in *Vekhi*

Americans are raised on the success ethic—work hard, get ahead, be successful in whatever you do. The success ethic, however, is alien to Russians who believe that it may be morally wrong to get ahead, particularly at the expense of others. Russians will not mind if their American acquaintances are successful, but they are likely to resent fellow Russians who "succeed." Belief in communism has eroded in Russia, but the egalitarian ethic still survives.

Egalitarianism is a social philosophy that advocates the removal of inequities among persons and a more equal distribution of benefits. In its Russian form it is not an invention of Communists but has its roots in the culture of the mir, which, as we have seen, represented village democracy, Russian style. Egalitarianism should not be confused with the American idea of fairness which implies equality of all people before the law and, in a more recent interpretation, equal opportunity.

The mir's governing body was an assembly composed of heads of households, including widowed women, and presided over by an elder. Before the introduction of currency, mir members were economically equal, and equality for members was considered more important than freedom. These agricultural communes, with their egalitarian lifestyle and distribution of material benefits, were seen by many Russian intellectuals as necessary to protect the simple peasants from the harsh competition of Western individualism. Individual rights, it was feared, would enable the strong to prosper but cause the weak to suffer. Others saw the mir as a form of agrarian socialism, the answer to Russia's striving for egalitarianism.

For much of Russian history peasants numbered close to 90 percent of the population. By 1990, due to forced industrialization, the figure had dropped to near 30 percent. But while the other two-thirds of the population today live in urban areas, most of today's city dwellers are only two or three generations removed from their ancestral villages. Their peasant past is still very much with them, and many of them still think in the egalitarian terms of the mir.

The Soviet state also thought in egalitarian terms. Its leveling of society revived the communal ethic of the mir on a national scale. Communism aimed to make a complete break with the past and create a new society, but its leaders could not escape from the heritage of the past. As British writer Geoffrey Hosking observes,

In some ways...the Soviet state has perpetuated the attitudes of the pre-1930 Russian village community. The expectation is still prevalent that the community will guarantee essentials in a context of comradely indigence just above the poverty line.[1]

Many aspects of Russian communism may indeed be traced to the mir. The meetings of the village assembly were lively, but decisions were usually unanimous and binding on all members. This provided a precedent for the Communist party's "democratic centralism," a practice under which issues were debated, decisions were made which all Party members were obliged to support, and opposition was prohibited.

Peasants could not leave the mir without an internal passport, issued only with the permission of their heads of household. This was a precursor, not only of Soviet (and tsarist) regulations denying citizens freedom of movement and resettlement within the country, but also of the practice of denying emigration to those who did not have parental permission. Under communism, the tapping of telephones and the perusal of private mail by the KGB must have seemed natural to leaders whose ancestors lived in a mir where the community was privy to the personal affairs of its members. And, in a society where the bulk of the population was tied to the land and restricted in movement, defections by Soviet citizens abroad were seen as treasonous.

Russians respect authority but are not intimidated by it. They regard themselves as coequal with others and are not shy about speaking up in public or asserting themselves in meetings. Nor are they hesitant about forcefully requesting things that they believe are rightly theirs or that they would like to possess.

Despite its egalitarian ethic, Old Russia also had an entrepreneurial tradition based in a small merchant class called *kupyechestvo*. Russian merchants established medieval trading centers, such as the city-state of Novgorod, which were independent and self-governing until absorbed by Muscovy in the late fifteenth century. Merchants explored and developed Siberia and played a major role in Russia's industrialization of the late nineteenth and early twentieth centuries.

Merchants were also Westernizers in the years between the revolutions of 1905 and 1917, endorsing social and legal reform, the rule of law, civil liberties, and broader educational opportunities. They rejected economic liberalism, however, and its emphasis on free trade in international exchange and free competition in the domestic economy, advocating state planning instead. And, as an additional link in the chain of continuity between the Old and New Russia, as Ruth Roosa has pointed out, merchants in the years prior to 1917 called for state plans of five, ten, and even fifteen years' duration embracing all aspects of economic life.[2]

Agriculture in Old Russia also had its entrepreneurs. Much of the land had been held in large estates by the crown, aristocracy, and landed gentry, but after the emancipation of the serfs in 1861, a small class of independent farmers began to appear. By 1917, on the eve of the revolution, some 10 percent of the peasants were independent farmers. The more enterprising and prosperous among them were called *kulaks* (fists) by their less successful and envious brethren who had remained in the mir. But the kulaks were ruthlessly eliminated and their land forcibly collectivized by the Communists in 1929-1930, a loss which contributed to the eventual failure of Soviet agriculture.

Since perestroika, privatization has been recognized as an essential component of economic reform. Legislation approved by the Russian republic in 1990 gives Russian citizens and foreign companies the right to own factories and other enterprises as well as other property in the republic.[3] New legislation also encourages "cooperatives," the new term for small, privately owned businesses. These include such enterprises as restaurants, shops, medical clinics, taxi service, engineering firms, and even public pay toilets, which fill consumer needs not met by the state economy. And in an effort to increase agricultural production, new legislation also permits private ownership of land, a move not yet widely accepted by peasants who are suspicious of the state's intentions and the local officials they must deal with as well as the permanence of the new legislation. Once burned, twice cautious! Sixty years of central planning and a command economy have taken their toll.

These measures, seen by younger people as solutions to Russia's economic ills, have been slow in gaining support among the general public, particularly the older generation. While there is a streak of individualism in many Russians, the entrepreneurial spirit of the businessman and independent farmer runs counter to Russian egalitarianism. Most Russians, it is often said, would rather bring other people down to their level than try to rise higher, a mentality known as *uravnilovka* (leveling).

The persistence of the egalitarian ethic in 1990 was explained by Leonid Shalagin, general director of a St. Petersburg association which promotes U.S.-Russian business ventures:

> Psychologically, people in the USSR aren't ready for even the concept of private ownership....There is a strong desire among Soviet citizens to deprive other people of their riches and to divide them among the population.[4]

The concept of reward tied to performance is also alien, notes Peter Cappelli, a professor at the Wharton School. After a trip to the Soviet Union in 1990, he reported:

> Some managers we spoke to were prepared to agree that rewards for employees might vary with the performance of the enterprises, but none felt that an individual's performance should influence his or her compensation. Indeed, the very notion that individual initiative is important is out of step with Soviet norms. The hostility sometimes directed by the general public against small-time entrepreneurs in farming or restaurants is based largely on the view that entrepreneurial activities are illegitimate.[5]

A 1991 public opinion poll by the Times Mirror Center for The People & The Press showed that Russians are deeply divided on the desirability of change to a free market economy. While a majority of those queried favored political pluralism—

free elections and a multiparty system—there was deep division over economic pluralism.[6]

When asked to choose between various socialist and capitalist alternatives for the future, 46 percent of Russians who were polled chose a socialist alternative compared to 40 percent who selected some form of capitalism. Most preferred democratic socialism (36 percent), while a Scandinavian form of capitalism was the second most popular choice (23 percent). Only 10 percent wanted the communism they have known in the past, and only 17 percent a free market form of capitalism. An overwhelming 79 percent thought heavy industry should be state-run.

In the survey, more support for the free market was evidenced by men, younger people, and the more affluent. Less support was shown by women, older people, and lower wage earners. This division between "fathers and sons" is a familiar theme in Russian literature—and in other cultures as well—and may well be a portent of the future.

In interpreting the results of the poll, it should be noted that Russian experience with the free market today is very limited, and public opinion is most likely shaped by experience with the so-called cooperatives and other private businesses that have sprung up since the reforms of perestroika.

As for the cooperatives, the survey showed that most Russians believe that the people who run them are having a bad effect on the way things are going in the country. Moreover, 45 percent thought the state should limit profits, and 46 percent thought that people who get ahead do so at the expense of others. Only 37 percent saw success as a consequence of some people having more ability than others.

"Opinions about capitalism generally and economic reforms," the Times Mirror report concluded, "reflect more deep seated values and beliefs. Deep-rooted feelings about egalitarianism and individualism are especially relevant."[7]

Public resentment is directed against those who have prospered under the economic reforms. Persons who establish small business enterprises are often regarded as speculators, and the higher prices they charge are resented even when they are for goods and services not provided by the state economy. The entrepreneurs of the new private sector are also seen as exploiters of the public. Many of the products they provide are made from materials siphoned—purchased illegally—from the state sector of the economy, thus aggravating existing shortages. Here lie the seeds of further social discord.

Caution and Conservatism

The slower you go, the further you'll get.

—Russian proverb

Living in a country that claimed to be socialist, Russians have been assumed by some Westerners to be radicals and challengers of the established order. In reality, they are more likely to be cautious and conservative defenders of the status quo. Their cruel climate, harsh history, and skeptical outlook on life have caused Russians to value stability, security, social order, and predictability, and to avoid risk. The tried and tested is preferred over the new and unknown, and with good reason.

Caution and conservatism are legacies of the Russian peasant past. As subsistence farmers barely eking out a living in small isolated villages, peasants had to contend not only with the vagaries of nature but also with the strictures of communal life, authoritarian fathers, all-powerful officials, and reproachful religious leaders. In a traditional agricultural society, stability was valued, and change came slowly. As Marshall Shulman of Columbia University says, "Russians feel obliged to defend their traditional values against the onslaught of the modern world."[8]

The experience of the twentieth century has given Russians no cause to moderate their caution. "Man-made catastrophies," writes Stephen F. Cohen of Princeton University, "have repeatedly victimized millions of ordinary [Russian] citizens and officials alike—the first European war, revolution, civil war, two great famines, forced collectivization, Stalin's terror, World War

II, and more." From these events, concludes Cohen, has come a conservatism which is "a real bond between state and society—and thus the main obstacle to change."[9]

Caution and conservatism can also be seen at the highest levels of government, where most of the leadership, including President Boris Yeltsin, is of peasant origin. Reflecting their peasant past, Russia's leaders will take advantage of every opportunity to advance their cause but will be careful to avoid undue risk.

The cautious approach was recommended by Mr. Gorbachev in a talk he gave in Washington during the June 1990 Summit. Noting that he preferred not to act precipitously in resolving international differences, Mr. Gorbachev advocated an approach that "…is more humane. That is to be very cautious, to consider a matter seven times, or even a hundred times before one takes a decision."[10] (In retrospect, Mr. Gorbachev proved to have been more daring in international affairs, where he achieved his greatest success, while his caution and equivocation at home led to his difficulties in domestic affairs.)

Americans, a nation of risk takers, will have their patience tested by Russian caution. Most Americans are descendants of immigrants who dared to leave the known of the Old World for the unknown of the New. In America risk takers have had the opportunity to succeed or to fail in the attempt. Indeed, risk is the quintessence of a market economy.

The opportunities of the New World, its social mobility and stability, have helped Americans to accentuate the positive. For Russians, geography and history have caused them to anticipate the negative.

Pessimism

In our cold winter each opening of the door is a repetition of dying. Russians do not fear death because every day is a struggle. It is a pity to die, and a pity not to die.

—Mark Davydov

This pessimistic outlook on life by Davydov, a contemporary Moscow poet, was given in response to my asking him what Americans should know to better understand Russians. Life has indeed been difficult for Russians. Weather, wars, violence, cataclysmic changes, and oppressive rule have made them pessimists.

Russian pessimism contrasts with American innocence and optimism. Americans expect things to go well and become upset when they do not. Russians expect things to go poorly and have learned to live with misfortune.

Americans are taught to "keep smiling," a trait that to Russians appears naive and even suspect. An American scholar recalls how he once brought shoes to a Moscow cobbler for repair. Entering the shop smiling, as he would at home, he presented his shoes to the cobbler. "What are you smiling at?" barked the cobbler angrily.

A Russian joke describes a pessimist as a realistic optimist. Americans will have to become realistic optimists in appraising prospects for their ventures in Russia.

When asked to explain the grounds for his pessimism, a Russian professor told me, "Our main concern, that which determines all our actions and feelings, is *strakh* (fear). The world is dangerous, and we must be careful."

Strakh will be encountered in many places but particularly among intellectuals whose hopes for reforms and a better future have been shattered several times, first by Khrushchev and more recently by Gorbachev. Americans should not be put off by this gloom and doom, nor should they attempt to make optimists of Russians. The best response is to express understanding and sympathy.

When asked how things are, a Russian is likely to reply *normalno* (normal), which might be translated as "not too bad." Translators Richard Lourie and Aleksei Mikhalev go further, describing normalno as "a wistful, ironic word, containing all the pain that came before and all of the hope of what might yet come to pass, the great dream of the present, a 'normal' society."[11]

Less in control of their lives than Americans, Russians feel caught up in the big sweeps of history where the individual does not count. As Lourie and Mikhalev say, the difference is simple and dramatic:

> For us, history is a subject, a black-and-white newsreel; for them it is a tank on their street, a search of their apartment by strangers with power. In the Soviet Union nearly every life has been touched directly, branded, by the great historical spasms of revolution, war and terror. For a Russian, repression always comes from the outside world....[12]

Glasnost and perestroika were exciting for Americans to follow from a distance. But to Russians, they were yet another historical spasm with attendant uncertainties about the future. In 1990, only 35 percent of Soviet citizens were satisfied with their lives (compared with 92 percent for Americans), according to a poll taken by the Soviet Academy of Sciences on behalf of the *Los Angeles Times*. The poll also disclosed that some two-thirds of those polled would be willing to accept painful economic reforms if they led to an improved standard of living. But if the reforms should fail, 49 percent said that the chances of a public revolt are either "very high" or "fairly high."[13]

During 1989, crime increased countrywide by 32 percent, according to official Soviet statistics. The largest increases were of violent and premeditated crimes, with thefts and robberies involving violence increasing by 170 percent. Assaults and murders rose by 38 percent and 31 percent respectively.[14] Muggings on Moscow streets are now a common occurrence at night.

Life expectancy for Soviet citizens in 1989 was 69.8 years (compared to 75 for Americans), which put the Soviet Union in thirty-second place among thirty-three developed nations.[15] Moreover, life expectancy for males was 64.8 years, and for females 73.6. These low figures are due, in part, to a high infant mortality rate, which in 1989 was officially reported as 22.2 per 1,000 live births.[16] Western experts, however, believe that infant mortality is actually higher, due to differences in methodology and reporting errors. One American expert, Murray Feshbach of Georgetown University, believes it may be as high as 33 to 35, which would make life expectancy much lower than reported.[17]

Many Russians believe that their country today is indeed on the verge of disaster—threatened by famine, energy shortages, political strife, ethnic warfare, revolution, and environmental degradation. Some Russians even speak of genetic degradation.

The best and brightest have traditionally been banished. In Old Russia independent thinkers were exiled to Siberia. Following the Bolshevik Revolution, the cream of Russia's elite was eliminated. Stalin's purges of the 1930s further decimated the intelligentsia, and today many of Russia's best are being lost through emigration. "The best of our people were exiled or killed in the 1920s and 1930s," a Russian psychologist told me. "Then Stalin altered the genetic future of Russia by eliminating our best. Today, the best of the Jews have emigrated. In our country only second- and third-raters remain."

One of those who left is Vladimir Voinovich, a popular and critically acclaimed writer. In 1975 Voinovich was forced to emigrate to the West after the KGB suggested to him that his future in the Soviet Union would be "unbearable." A satirist in the tradition of Gogol, Voinovich has described how Americans and Russians react differently to his writing. "Russians and Americans," he writes, "read my books in very different ways. Americans usually say they are funny. Russians say...they are very gloomy, dark."[18] This gloomy and dark side of the Russian character explains the bittersweet humor that is native to Russia, and the "good news, bad news" jokes. (Voinovich later returned to Russia and now divides his time between Moscow and Munich.)

Russian pessimism can also be infectious, and Americans who have worked with them for many years are vulnerable to the virus. Llewellyn Thompson, twice American ambassador to Moscow, was asked on his retirement in 1968 to name his greatest accomplishment. "That I didn't make things any worse," replied the veteran diplomat.[19]

Despite their pessimism, there is an admirable durability about Russians, a hardy people who have more than proven their ability to endure severe deprivation and suffer lengthy hardships. Tibor Szamuely has written of "...the astonishing durability of...certain key social and political institutions, traditions, habits, and attitudes, their staying power, their essential stability amidst the turbulent currents of violent change, chaotic upheaval, and sudden innovation."[20]

One might wonder what has sustained Russia for more than a thousand years. "The strength of the people," explains Mstislav Rostropovich, "is the strength of Russia."[21]

Extremes and Contradictions

> Contradiction is...the essence of Russia. West and East, Pacific and Atlantic, Arctic and tropics, extreme cold and extreme heat, prolonged sloth and sudden feats of energy, exaggerated cruelty and exaggerated kindness, ostentatious wealth and dismal squalor, violent xenophobia and uncontrollable yearning for contact with the foreign world, vast power and the most abject slavery, simultaneous love and hate for the same objects.... The Russian does not reject these contradictions. He has learned to live with them, and in them. To him, they are the spice of life.
> —George F. Kennan, Memoirs

President Harry Truman once quipped that he was looking for a one-armed economist because all his economic advisers concluded their advice to him by saying, "...but, on the other hand." Americans, with their proclivity for rational consistency, seek clear and precise responses. They also prefer a middle road that avoids contradictions and extremes.

Russians, by contrast, have a reputation for extremes. When emotions are displayed, they are spontaneous and strong. Russian hospitality can be overwhelming, friendship all encompassing, compassion deep, loyalty long lasting, drinking heavy, cel-

ebrations boisterous, obsession with security paranoid, and violence vicious. With Russians, it is often all or nothing. Halfway
measures simply will not suffice.

"The Anglo-Saxon instinct," writes George F.
Kennan, America's distinguished diplomatist and historian, "is to attempt to smooth away contradictions, to reconcile opposing
elements, to achieve something in the nature of an acceptable
middle ground as a basis for life." The Russian, continues
Kennan, tends to deal only in extremes, "...and he is not particularly concerned to reconcile them."[22] The American mind,
concludes Kennan, will not understand Russia until it accepts
that

> because a proposition is true, the opposite of that proposition is not
> false. It must agree never to entertain a proposition about the
> Russian world without seeking, and placing in apposition to it, its
> inevitable and indispensable opposite. Then it must agree to regard
> both as legitimate, valid conceptions...to understand that Russian
> life at any given moment is not the common expression of harmo-
> nious integrated elements, but a precarious and evershifting equi-
> librium between numbers of conflicting forces.... Right and wrong,
> reality and unreality, are determined in Russia, not by any God, not
> by any innate nature of things, but simply by men themselves. Here
> men determine what is true and what is false.[23]

Russian extremes and contradictions have also been described
by Yevgeny Yevtushenko, one of Russia's most popular contemporary poets: "I am thus and not thus, I am industrious and lazy,
determined and shiftless. I am...shy and impudent, wicked and
good; in me is a mixture of everything from the west to the east,
from enthusiasm to envy...."[24]

Human feelings count for much in Russia, and those who do
not share the depth of these feelings—Americans among
them—will be considered cold and distant. When Russians
open their souls to someone, it is a sign of acceptance and
sharing. Americans may have to drop their stiff upper lips and
open their souls too.

The Russian Soul

> The famous 'Russian soul' was to no small extent the product of this agonizing uncertainty regarding Russia's proper geographical, social, and spiritual position in the world, the awareness of a national personality that was split between East and West.
>
> —Tibor Szamuely, *The Russian Tradition*

Andrei Amalryk, the Russian political dissident, was in trouble with the authorities for most of his adult life. During a sentence to political exile in faraway Magadan, just across the Bering Strait from Alaska, Amalryk encountered by chance the man who had denounced him to the authorities. The denouncer expressed regret, asked forgiveness, and suggested they have a drink. After consuming a bottle of vodka—which got both of them drunk—the man became even more remorseful and asked Amalryk what he could do to make amends. Amalryk suggested that the man write an account of what he had done. The denouncer wrote out a confession of how he had succumbed to KGB pressure and falsified his testimony, signed it, and presented it to Amalryk with great emotion. A few hours later, however, sober and no longer remorseful, he asked that it be returned to him and, when Amalryk refused, even offered to buy it back.[25]

Russkaya dusha (Russian soul) can turn up suddenly in the most unexpected places, and just as suddenly disappear. Just when Americans believe that Russians are about to get down to serious business, they can become decidedly emotional and unbusinesslike.

Dusha is well known in the arts, where it manifests itself as emotion, sentimentality, exuberance, energy, theatricality, flamboyant virtuosity, and bravura technique. Dusha, however, transcends the arts; it is the essence of Russian behavior.

A romantic ethos, dusha appeals to feeling rather than fact, sentiment over certainty, suffering instead of satisfaction, and nostalgia for the past as opposed to the reality of the present. In a broader sense, dusha is also a reaffirmation of the purity of traditional Russian values against the encroachment of Western enlightenment, rationalism, and secularism, especially in things cultural. Russian dusha is derided in the West as an invention of artists, composers, and writers. If dusha ever really existed, this argument goes, it was the product of a traditional agricultural society which had very little in material goods to offer. In a modern industrial society, dusha is quickly forgotten and Russians become as realistic, practical, materialistic, and unromantic as Americans.

The truth lies somewhere in between. Russians have a rich spirituality that does indeed contrast with American rationalism, materialism, and pragmatism. Russians suffer but seem to enjoy their suffering. Obsessed with ideas, their conversation is weighty and lengthy. The rational and pragmatic approach does not do for them. More often, it is personal relations, feelings, and traditional values that determine a course of action. Americans are more likely to depend on the cold facts and to do what works.

As Tatyana Tolstaya, one of Russia's leading young writers, says,

> Logical categories are inapplicable to the soul. But Russian sensitivity, permeating the whole culture, doesn't want to use logic— logic is seen as dry and evil, logic comes from the devil—the most important thing is sensation, smell, emotion, tears, mist, dreams, and enigma.[26]

Belief in village virtues is still strong—self-sacrifice, sense of duty, compassion, the importance of family, love of nature. These aspects of the Russian soul are again the themes of writers who glorify peasant life and encourage a renaissance of traditional Russian values.

"In Russian culture, emotion is assigned an entirely positive value," writes Tolstaya, "...the more a person expresses his emotions, the better, more sincere, and more 'open' he is."[27] The Russian mentality, she believes, has penetrated to some degree all corners of the country, "often not for the best." Dusha is described by Tolstaya as

> sensitivity, reverie, imagination, an inclination to tears, compassion, submission mingled with stubbornness, patience that permits survival in what would seem to be unbearable circumstances, poetry, mysticism, fatalism, a penchant for walking the dark, humid back streets of consciousness, introspection, sudden, unmotivated cruelty, mistrust of rational thought, fascination with the word—the list could go on and on—all these qualities that have frequently been attributed to the "Slavic soul."[28]

In the final decade of the twentieth century, does the Russian soul still exist? When asked this question, a Moscow psychiatrist told me, "The real Russia is being diluted by Westernization and Sovietization. Soviet is not Russian. To see the real Russia, visit a village, a church. The Russian soul still exists. It is the essence of the Russian person."

This essence of the Russian person has many aspects that Americans can respect and admire. As Northwestern University professor Irwin Weil puts it:

> Russians maintain their integrity in a way that conforms to their inner notion of what a human being should be, in a manner they consider proper, and with an honesty and decency that I have seldom seen anywhere else in the world. Above all, they have an appreciation for *tselnost* (wholeness, complete commitment) and faith, no matter what that faith may be related to. To be a real human being, one must maintain that full commitment and respect it in other people as well. In this sense, it makes no difference to them whether the other person is a Marxist or a reactionary."[29]

Russians are sensitive to their own feelings and to those of others as well. Weil recalls how Cuban students at Moscow State University, during the Cuban missile crisis of 1962, placed signs calling President Kennedy an "s.o.b." above the doors to their dormitory rooms. Russian students complained to the student council that the signs were offensive to American students at the university, and the Cubans were ordered by the student council to remove them. On the death of President Kennedy in 1963, Weil received three letters from Russian friends expressing their personal condolences.[30]

Other examples of Russian soul are the courage and moral strength of Russia's two most prominent political dissidents, Andrei Sakharov and Aleksandr Solzhenitsyn, in the face of KGB harassment and persecution. Their politics differed— Sakharov was a Westernizer and Solzhenitsyn is a Slavophile— but both were awarded Nobel prizes, the former for peace, the latter for literature.

Sakharov, the celebrated nuclear physicist who helped to develop the Soviet hydrogen bomb, suffered seven years of internal exile in Gorky for his outspoken opposition to the Soviet war in Afghanistan. Returning to Moscow in 1986, ailing but unbroken in spirit, a year after Mr. Gorbachev's advent to power, he continued his struggle for human rights and led the democratic opposition until his untimely death in 1989.

Solzhenitsyn in 1971, after a search of his house by the KGB during which one of his friends was brutally beaten, had the courage to send an indignant open letter of protest to Yuri Andropov, KGB head at the time. In his letter, Solzhenitsyn demanded from Andropov "...the public identification of all the intruders, their punishment as criminals, and a public explanation of this incident. Otherwise I can only conclude that they were sent by *you.*"[31] Solzhenitsyn, author of *The Gulag Archipelago*, an exposé of Stalin's slave labor camps, survived his challenge to the KGB but was exiled from the Soviet Union in 1974.

The Russian soul is still spirited as the twentieth century draws to a close. Old virtues endure—respect for parents, deference to old age, regard for learning. Students hang on the words of their professors. Grateful audiences present flowers to musical and theatrical performers. Before vacating a home where they have lived for some time, Russians will sit quietly for a minute or two, reflecting on the events they have experienced there. Even in the postindustrial age, Russians demonstrate that emotions and personal feelings still matter.

Big Is Beautiful

> In its grandiose schemes which were always on a worldwide scale, communism makes use of the Russian disposition for making plans and castle-building which had hitherto no scope for practical application.
>
> —Nikolai Berdyaev, *The Origin of Russian Communism*

"Sire, every thing is done on a large scale in this country — every thing is colossal."[32] So spoke the Marquis de Custine, addressing Tsar Nicholas in Petersburg in 1839 at the start of his travels through Russia. The French aristocrat was moved by the grand scale of "this colossal empire," as he described it in his four-volume *Russia in 1839*.

Modern-day travelers to Russia will also encounter colossal sights. At Moscow's Kremlin, Intourist guides point with pride to the Tsar Cannon—cast in 1586, with a bore of 36 inches and weight of 44 tons. Nearby is the Tsar Bell—20 feet high and, at 200 tons, the heaviest in the world.

Soviet leaders continued this "colossalism." The Palace of Soviets, a Stalin project of the 1930s, was to have been the tallest building in the world, dwarfing the Empire State Building and the Eiffel Tower. The Kremlin's Palace of Congresses, the huge hall known to Western TV viewers as the site of mass meetings, seats 6,000 and is one of the world's largest conference halls. Its snack bar can feed 3,000 people in ten minutes, thanks to the many Russian grandmothers who staff its buffet. Moscow's Hotel Rossiya, the world's largest, can accommodate 6,000 guests in 3,200 rooms.

In Volgograd, formerly Stalingrad and the site of a great battle with Germany in World War II, a victorious Mother

Russia, the largest full-figure statue in the world, towers 282 feet over the battlefield. The Soviet supersonic transport, the first SST to enter passenger service, was far larger than the Anglo-French Concorde. And when McDonald's opened its first hamburger restaurant in Russia in 1990—only a few blocks from Moscow's Kremlin—it was the largest McDonald's in the world, with a capacity of 900 and serving 40,000 customers a day.

Russians are impressed with size and numbers, and much that they do is on a grand scale. This is not unusual for such a vast country. Russians think and act big, and they do not do things in a half-hearted way. Nor are these traits uniquely Russian. Americans, accustomed to wide open spaces and with an expansive outlook on life, also think big.

Big also describes the Russian military which was the largest regular armed force in the world. The Russians had the biggest missiles, submarines, and aircraft. Their numerical superiority over most U.S. equivalents was overwhelming and was used by the Pentagon to justify requests for larger military budgets.

To be sure, the United States must consider foreign capabilities to determine the forces needed to counter them. But when motives are sought for the Russian advantage in conventional forces, all possibilities should be considered. Did the Russians believe the United States was preparing to launch an attack? Did they seek quantitative superiority to counter the U.S. qualitative lead? Did they build big because they did not have the technology to build small? These are all possible explanations that should be considered in analyzing their motives. Another explanation, however, is simply that Russians are impressed with size and numbers. For Russians, big is beautiful.

Russia's grandiose plans have at times been realized, and at other times not. The Tsar Bell was too heavy and was neither hung nor rung. The Tsar Cannon was too big to fire. The Palace of Soviets was abandoned after the foundation proved incapable of supporting the structure, and the site today is occupied by an outdoor swimming pool—one of the largest in Europe, of course. The Russian SST had major design problems and was shelved after several crashes, including one at the prestigious Paris Air Show.

And what should be said of the current reforms, the most recent of many attempts to reform Russia? The objective this time is to modernize Russia, to make it more competitive with the West, and to maintain its superpower status.

The reforms have been described as a task of gargantuan dimensions. Others see them as the most recent instance of Russian frenzied effort following a period of stagnation.

Will reform succeed, or is it merely the latest example of Russians thinking too big? History tells us to believe the latter.

Mother Russia, the Other Russia

> Oh, Russian women, draft horses of the nation!
> —Andrei Sinyavsky, Goodnight!

Some nations are called a fatherland, others a motherland. Russia is clearly a motherland. Rodina, the word for homeland, is feminine, and Mother Russia is the symbol of the nation. In this motherland, women are strong, hard-working, nurturing, long-suffering, and the true heroes of Russia.

Russian literature, writes Hingley, again and again gives us situations

> in which a beautiful, strong, well-integrated, decisive young woman becomes erotically implicated with some spineless, dithering pipsqueak of a man who invariably emerges discredited from the involvement. In fiction of the totalitarian [Soviet] period the clash between strong female and weak male is more than ever in vogue, and has been well analyzed in terms which appropriately recall the life-cycle of the spider.[33]

The Bolsheviks professed to liberate women and give them full equality with men, and in the 1920s Russian women enjoyed an equality under law unequaled anywhere else in the world. On this point Soviet law was explicit. Article 35 of the 1977 Constitution declared:

> Women and men have equal rights in the USSR…ensured by according women equal access with men to education and vocational and professional training, equal opportunities in employment, remuneration and promotion, and in social and political, and cultural activity.[34]

In practice, women are recognized but unrewarded. A state that claimed to have given all power to the people did in fact give power to only a few, and almost all of them have been men. Since the start of the Soviet state, only three women were named to the ruling Politburo of the Communist party and almost none to high positions in the military and diplomatic corps. To be sure, the first woman ambassador of any country was an early Bolshevik, Aleksandra Kollontai. She was named Soviet Minister to Norway in 1923 but only after her ardent feminism and advocacy of free love put her on a collision course with Party leaders at home.

Some 90 percent of Russian women are in the work force, where they occupy mostly secondary positions. Three-fourths of all medical doctors are women, and they are well represented in the professions but are seldom found in supervisory or management posts. Full gender equality in the work force is found only in the lowest paying jobs: women work as members of construction crews, farm laborers, street sweepers, and snow shovelers. However, while few women occupy high government positions, they are one-half of all members of local soviets (city councils), performing the day-to-day work of local government.

Women in Russia, says Hingley, possess greater stamina and force of character than men, and in the low- and mid-level political positions to which they are confined, they "…constitute a bulwark of a system which might conceivably fall apart were it left in the exclusive custodianship of the relatively easygoing Russian male."[35]

Women—the bulwark of the system and perhaps the reason why it keeps going—actually work two shifts: one at the workplace and the other at home where they put in another forty hours a week at the traditional duties of wife, mother, and homemaker, but without the labor-saving appliances common in the West and without much help from their husbands. Russian researchers believe that the amount of household labor differs only slightly from the labor expended in the entire public economy.[36]

Mr. Gorbachev, in his book *Perestroika*, says it is imperative to more actively involve women in the management of the economy, cultural development, and public life, and to promote them to administrative posts. However, when discussing problems caused by weakened family ties, Mr. Gorbachev notes that heated debates are being held "…about the question of what we should do to make it possible for women to return to their purely womanly mission."[37]

This "purely womanly mission" has been frustrated by recent history. Forty million Soviet men died in the three cataclysmic events of the Soviet era—the collectivization of agriculture, the political purges, and World War II—creating a severe shortage of men for two generations of women. Moreover, the mortality rate for men is three times that of women in all age groups over twenty, largely due to alcoholism and related accidents and illnesses.[38] This explains why there are so many *babushkas* (grandmothers) in Russia and so few grandfathers.

Attitudes on birth control stem from traditional Russian conservatism as well as from the ideological considerations of a male-dominated leadership which seeks to stabilize the family and increase the birthrate. Most families, however, avoid having a second child, mainly because of limited housing space, especially in the cities. Birth control devices, nevertheless, are either not available or are primitive and in short supply, and family planning information is hard to come by.

Abortion is the common form of birth control. According to conservative estimates, the average woman has two and one-half to three abortions during her lifetime. If Islamic women are not included, the average rises to four or more.[39] A few more facts will help to explain the condition of women in the society. Items of feminine hygiene taken for granted in the West are not always available in Russia. (Visitors are advised to bring whatever items they may need as well as common medicines and antibiotics.) One of every three marriages ends in divorce (compared with one of every two in the United States). Promiscuity is common but exists side by side with extreme modesty. While glasnost lowered official barriers to nudity and sexually explicit scenes in films, television, and theater, most Russians of the middle and older generations feel uncomfortable with these new liberties, and sex is not a subject for public discussion. Prudery prevails. A woman, for example, will never ask a man for directions to the ladies' room; the man would be even more embarrassed than the woman. Feminism, like many other movements originating in the West, has been late in reaching Russia. Today, independent women's groups are springing up around the country, but feminism is not yet a mass movement.

Women, however, depend on and support each other to a remarkable degree. They have networks of trusted and lifelong friends who share scarce goods, help each other with the daily hassles of living, and can be called upon in a crisis.

How does all this affect Western women traveling to Russia on business? One American woman, a veteran of many visits there, warns that Russian men will turn on the charm but their basic attitude toward a female visitor will be patronizing, and the Western woman will have to prove herself to her male counterparts before she will be taken seriously. Initially, her professional qualifications will be regarded with skepticism.

The importance of professional qualifications is emphasized by Nancy Lubin of Carnegie Mellon University, a frequent visitor to Russia. Dr. Lubin advises American women to be well grounded in their fields of interest, to know what they want to accomplish, and not to be overly concerned about Russian male attitudes toward women.[40]

Another American woman scholar with long experience in Russia suggests a few stratagems that may help women to gain recognition from Russian professional contacts. An expensive-looking business card (bilingual preferred) will attract attention, as will an advanced academic degree or title. Name-dropping will likewise impress. Also helpful may be letters sent in advance by prominent persons vouching for the visitor.

Sex may play another role in U.S.-Russian contacts. Americans, male as well as female, may find that they are objects of considerable interest from the opposite sex. Before becoming romantically involved, however, they should understand that it may be their passport rather than their person that is the principal attraction. As a Russian joke puts it, an American is not just a future spouse but a means of transportation (from Russia).

Messianism

> The Occident disappears, everything collapses, everything totters in a general conflagration: the Europe of Charlemagne and the Europe of the treaties of 1815, the papacy of Rome and all the kingdoms of the West, Catholicism and Protestantism, faith long lost and reason reduced to absurdity. Order becomes henceforth impossible, freedom becomes henceforth impossible, and Occidental civilization commits suicide on top of all the ruins accumulated by it.... And when we see rise above this immense wreck this even more immense Eastern Empire like the Ark of the Covenant, who could doubt its mission...
>
> —Fyodor Tyutchev, *The Rock of Refuge*

Tyutchev, a Russian diplomat and poet, wrote these words in 1848 in response to the liberal revolutions sweeping Western Europe in that year. He saw Western civilization as disintegrating while Russian civilization, morally and spiritually superior, was rising.

Messianism is still alive in Russia today, particularly among intellectuals, on the left as well as the right, who share a belief and pride in Russia as a great power with a special mission in the world. Economist Mikhail F. Antonov, for example, in an interview with the *New York Times Magazine*, showed that Tyutchev's belief in Russia's messianic mission and superiority is still very much alive in the 1990s.

"Let other countries surpass us in the technology of computer production," says Antonov, "but only we can provide an answer to the question: Why? For whose sake? We are the only legitimate heirs to the great, spiritual Russian culture. The saving of the world will come from Soviet Russia."[41]

Tyutchev and Antonov epitomize Russian thinkers, past and present, who seek to excuse her material backwardness by acclaiming her correctness of cause, spiritual superiority, and messianic mission.

A similar view was espoused by a contemporary Russian philosopher when he was asked about Russia's role in the world. "Russia is European on the surface," he told me, "but deep inside it is Asian, and our link between Europe and Asia is the Russian soul. Russia's mission is to unite Europe and Asia."

Such views are not unknown to Americans, who at times have also believed that they have something special to bring to the less fortunate—Christianity to heathens, democracy to dictatorships, and the free market to state-run economies. In his State of the Union message of 1991, President George Bush also sounded a note of messianism:

> For two centuries, America has served the world as an inspiring example of freedom and democracy. For generations, America has led the struggle to preserve and extend the blessings of liberty. And today, in a rapidly changing world, American leadership is indispensable.... But we also know why the hopes of humanity turn to us. We are Americans: we have a unique responsibility to do the hard work of freedom.[42]

Americans who believe in their own superiority and mission should be sensitive to Russian messianism and fears for the future. If Russia should lose her great-power status, Russians fear that other countries will no longer give them the respect they are due and Russia will lose her influence in the world. Russia's desperate economic situation, moreover, is a cause for embarrassment, and her need for foreign aid a public humiliation. In the 1990s Russians do indeed need aid from abroad, but they do not wish to appear as beggars seeking charity. Those who are able to provide such assistance should respect Russian sensitivities and avoid appearing condescending.

Along with messianism, there is also a Russian tendency to blame others for their misfortunes, and with a certain logic. If Russians are indeed the chosen people and have a monopoly on truth, then others must be the cause of their misfortunes.

Freemasons and Jews, among others, have been blamed in the past for Russia's troubles. In our time, some nationalities that sought secession from the Soviet Union have been accused of impeding the development of democracy by fueling nationalism in the Russian heartland. And with nationalism resurgent, Jews are again being blamed, this time for having imposed communism on Russia. As Sergei Stankevich, a political advisor to Yeltsin, explains, "Antisemitism, our social disease for decades, always reemerges in times of crisis."[43]

Rebellion and Revolt

> God defend you from the sight of a Russian rebellion in all its ruthless stupidity.
>
> —Aleksandr Pushkin, *The Captain's Daughter*

The patience of Russians sometimes wears thin and they rebel. History is replete with rebellions of serfs against masters, peasants against gentry, Cossacks against lords, nobles against princes, and Communists against commissars—usually with mindless destruction and wanton cruelty. There is also a record of revolt from within—palace revolutions—in the time of general secretaries as well as tsars, as Mr. Gorbachev learned in August 1991 when a hard-line junta attempted to seize power in Moscow.

Conspiracies, coups, insurrections, ethnic warfare, and national independence movements all reflect the instabilities and inequities of Russian society and its resistance to change. When peaceful evolution is not viable, revolution becomes inevitable. Russians have long been seen as submissive to authority, politically passive, and unswerving in policy. But when the breaking point is reached, the submissive citizen spurns authority, the docile worker strikes, the passive person becomes politically active, and rigid policies are reversed almost overnight.

Such a point was reached in the late 1980s when the Soviet Union experienced food shortages, crippling strikes, a deteriorating economy, nationality unrest, ethnic warfare, movements for sovereignty or independence by the republics, and inept government responses to two major catastrophes—the Chernobyl nuclear disaster and the Armenian earthquake. More such calamities are expected in the 1990s.

In reaction to these events, voters of the Russian Republic rebelled in 1991. Given a choice, they rejected the candidates of communism and chose as their president Boris Yeltsin and his program of decentralization, democracy, and economic reform. Yeltsin thus became the first freely elected leader in Russian history.

In August 1991 Russians again rebelled, taking to the streets in a massive protest that helped bring down the old guard junta that had attempted to seize power.

Westernizers and Slavophiles

> To Russia, in its hunger for civilization, the West seemed "the land of miracles"...
> —Thomas Masaryk, *The Spirit of Russia*

Russia's love-hate relationship with Europe has given rise to two schools of thought—Westernizers and Slavophiles. Both are regarded as Russian patriots, but they have held opposing views on how Russia should relate to the West.

Westernizers, recognizing Russia's backwardness, sought to borrow from the West in order to modernize. They saw Russia as a political entity that would benefit from Western enlightenment, rationalism, technology, manufacturing, and the growth of a middle class. Among the Westernizers were political reformers, Europeanizers, liberals, and socialists.

Slavophiles also sought to borrow from the West but were determined, at the same time, to protect and preserve Russia's unique cultural values and traditions. They rejected individualism and regarded the Church, rather than the state, as Russia's leading historical and moral force. Admirers of agricultural life, they were critical of urban development and industrialization. Slavophiles, moreover, sought to preserve the mir in order to prevent the growth of a Russian proletariat. They opposed socialism as alien to Russia and preferred Russian mysticism to Western rationalism. Among the Slavophiles were philosophical conservatives, nationalists, and the Church.

The controversy between Westernizers and Slavophiles has appeared in many forms in Russian history. As Seton-Watson has pointed out, it divided Russian socialism between Marxists and Populists, Russian Marxism between Mensheviks and Bolsheviks, and Bolshevism between opponents and followers of Stalin.[44] Another way of putting it, the controversy has been between those who believed in Europe and those who believed in Russia.

In our time, the old conflict continues between supporters and opponents of reform, between modernizers and traditionalists. Today's nationalists, seeking to preserve Russia's faith and harmony, are ideological descendants of the Slavophiles. Stanislav Kunyaev, leader of a delegation of Russian writers that visited the United States in 1990, says that he and his colleagues are "…linked by the idea of a Russian renaissance," a renewal of Russian culture and spirituality.[45]

To such Slavophiles, the moral basis of society takes priority over individual rights and material progress, a view held today by many Russians, non-Communist as well as Communist. As

Aleksandr Solzhenitsyn, a modern-day Slavophile, has said from his self-imposed seclusion in Vermont, fifteen years after his forced exile from the Soviet Union:

> There is technical progress [in the West], but this is not the same thing as the progress of humanity as such…. In Western civilization—which used to be called Western-Christian, but now might better be called Western-Pagan—along with the development of intellectual life and science there has been a loss of the serious moral basis of society. During these 300 years of Western civilization, there has been a sweeping away of duties and an expansion of rights…the only thing we have been developing is rights, rights, rights, at the expense of duty.[46]

This school of thought, epitomized by Solzhenitsyn, has given Russia a superiority complex toward the West in things ethereal, and an inferiority complex in matters material. The West is seen as spiritually impoverished and decadent, Russia as morally rich and virtuous.

----

[1]Geoffrey Hosking, *The Awakening of the Soviet Union* (Cambridge: Harvard University Press, 1990), 132.

[2]Ruth Amende Roosa, "Russian Industrialists Look to the Future: Thoughts on Economic Development, 1906-17," *Essays in Russian and Soviet History*, edited by John Shelton Curtiss (New York: Columbia University Press, 1963), 198-218.

[3]*Report on the USSR 3*, no. 1 (4 January 1991): 63.

[4]Leonid Shalagin, "Doing Business with the USSR," *Freedom at Issue* (July-August 1990): 20.

[5]Peter Cappelli, "Sorry, Perestroika Isn't Enough," *Wall Street Journal*, 6 August 1990.

[6]"Attitudes That Bear on Economic Reform in the U.S.S.R., A Preliminary Report," Times Mirror Center for The People & The Press, Washington, D.C., 28 July 1991.

[7]Ibid., 3.

[8]Marshall Shulman, in Face-to-Face lecture at the Carnegie Endowment for International Peace, Washington, D.C., 12 February 1989.

[9]Stephen F. Cohen, *Rethinking the Soviet Experience* (New York: Oxford University Press, 1985), 148.

[10]*New York Times*, 1 June 1990.

[11]Richard Lourie and Aleksei Mikhalev, "Why You'll Never Have Fun in Russian," *New York Times Book Review* (18 June 1989): 38.

[12]Ibid., 38.

[13]*Los Angeles Times*, 1 June 1990.

[14]D. J. Peterson, "Goskomstat Report on Social Conditions in 1989," *Report on the USSR* 2, no. 6 (9 February 1990): 5.

[15]Federal Center for Disease Control, reported in *New York Times*, 7 April 1990.

[16]Peterson, "Goskomstat Report," 5.

[17]Murray Feshbach, Professor of Demography, Georgetown University. Interview with author, February 1990.

[18]*New York Times*, 28 Nov. 1989.

[19]Llewellyn Thompson, in his final briefing for American correspondents prior to his departure from Moscow in 1968, a meeting which the author attended.

[20]Tibor Szamuely, *The Russian Tradition* (New York: McGraw-Hill, 1974), 6.

[21]Mstislav Rostropovich, *Soldiers of Music: Rostropovich Returns to Russia*, 1990. PBS television film.

[22]George F. Kennan, *Memoirs, 1925-1950* (Boston: Little, Brown and Company, 1967), 528.

[23]Ibid., 529.

[24]Yevgeny Yevtushenko, *Literaturnaya Gazeta*, (Moscow) 7 April 1958, quoted by Klaus Mehnert in *Soviet Man and his World* (New York: Frederick A. Praeger, 1961), 30.

[25]Andrei Amalryk, *Notes of a Revolutionary*, translated by Guy Daniels (New York: Knopf, 1982), 271. Additional details are from an interview by the author with Alfred Friendly, Jr., who heard the story firsthand from Amalryk.

[26]Tatyana Tolstaya, "Notes from Underground," *New York Review of Books* 37, translated by Jamey Gambrell (31 May 1990): 4.

[27]Ibid.

[28]Ibid.

[29]Irwin Weil. Interview with author, 4 February 1991.

[30]Ibid.

[31]Aleksandr I. Solzhenitsyn, *The Oak and the Calf, Sketches of*

Literary Life in the Soviet Union (New York: Harper and Row, 1975), 497-98.

[32]Marquis de Custine, *Empire of the Czar, A Journey Through Eternal Russia* (New York: Doubleday, Anchor Books, 1989), 183.

[33]Ronald Hingley, *The Russian Mind* (New York: Charles Scribner's Sons, 1977), 189.

[34]*Constitution (Fundamental Law) of the Union of Soviet Socialist Republics* (Moscow: Novosti, 1977), 38.

[35]Hingley, *Russian Mind*, 188.

[36]Vladimir Shlapentokh, *Love, Marriage, and Friendship in the Soviet Union* (New York: Praeger Publishers, 1984), 189.

[37]Mikhail Gorbachev, *Perestroika, New Thinking for Our Country and the World* (New York: Harper and Row, 1987), 116-17.

[38]Shlapentokh, *Love, Marriage, and Friendship*, 186.

[39]Murray Feshbach, Professor of Demography, Georgetown University. Interview with author, February 1990.

[40]Nancy Lubin. Interview with author, 9 March 1991.

[41]Mikhail F. Antonov, quoted by Bill Keller, "Yearning For An Iron Hand," *New York Times Magazine*, 28 Jan. 1990, 19.

[42]*New York Times*, 30 Jan. 1991.

[43]Sergei Stankevich. Talk at the National Endowment for Democracy, Washington, D.C., 8 May 1990.

[44]Hugh Seton-Watson, *The Decline of Imperial Russia, 1855-1914* (New York: Frederick A. Praeger, 1952), 24.

[45]*New York Times*, 18 April 1990.

[46]*Time*, 24 July 1989, 61.

State and Society

With the mind alone Russia cannot be understood,
No ordinary yardstick spans her greatness;
She stands alone, unique—
In Russia one can only believe.

—Fyodor Tyutchev[1]

The Russian Heritage

If men could foresee the future, they would still behave as they do now.

—Russian proverb

"I have seen the future and it works," wrote an American writer after visiting Russia in 1919. This euphoric vision, attributed to Lincoln Steffens, we now know was twice mistaken. The Soviet state did not portend the future, and Soviet society did not work.

To be sure, state and society were turned upside down by the Great October Revolution—as Communists term the Bolshevik seizure of power in 1917. The small, French-speaking elite that had ruled Russia was removed from power by confiscation of land and property, exile, and outright murder. The new ruling class, in theory, was to be workers and peasants, represented by local Soviets (councils) and guided by the Communist party. In practice, however, after Stalin had eliminated his rivals, one autocracy was replaced by another.

Building on the utopian dreams of generations of Russian thinkers, the Bolsheviks planned to create a new state and society—and even a new "Soviet person"—that would solve all of Old Russia's problems. By applying the principles of what they called "scientific socialism"—a Western import—they would establish the new order by nationalizing production, instituting central planning, abolishing private property, and redistributing wealth according to the Marxist maxim, "From each according to his ability, to each according to his work." And all this was to be accomplished under the direction of the Communist party, which, as the Soviet Constitution put it, would be "the leading and guiding force of Soviet society and the nucleus of its political system."

The Bolsheviks, however, found themselves heirs to many relics of Old Russia—a vast multinational empire dominated by Russians, governed from its center, and ruled by coercion rather than law; a state-imposed ideology that set standards for citizen behavior; a bureaucracy that was arrogant, corrupt, and incompetent; the priority of the community over the individual; a pervasive censorship; suspicion of dissidents and others who thought differently; and a ubiquitous secret police to enforce the state's will.

Americans who rail against the intrusions of government in their lives should try to imagine a state and society that is run like a huge corporation without competitors, a monopoly controlled and managed by insiders. In this corporation individual rights are subordinated to the greater communal good, as seen by the board of directors, whose decisions are final.

America also had a revolution, but it did not turn society upside down. America's society was homogeneous, mostly of English origin at the time of the revolution, numbering only four million, and living in relative proximity along the Atlantic coast. The system of governance, based on English common law, economic liberalism, and individual rights, did portend the future, and it worked. America's models were England and Western enlightenment. The models for Russia were Byzantium and Mongol rule.

Russia today, neither European nor Asian, is beset with contradictions. In many ways it is a developed country, with heavy industry, high technology, world-class science, awesome military strength, and nuclear power. In other ways it is a developing country, with poverty, ignorance, inefficiency, low productivity, poor public health, and a primitive infrastructure. It is this Third-World Russia that is being coaxed reluctantly into the modern world.

Experts, both Russian and Western, are divided on the prospects for reform in Russia. But whatever the results, they can be expected to reflect the values and views that are rooted in the Russian past.

"One of the major features of Soviet culture and the Soviet way of life and one of the secrets of its survival," writes Richard Stites, "is its ability to retain certain key elements of the deep Russian past, modified and harnessed to the use of the regime."[2]

Statism

Who serves the Tsar cannot serve the people.

—Russian proverb

Russians have a deep and abiding suspicion of government. In the past their governments have served rulers rather than the ruled. Until Russia's free elections of 1991, democratic governance was experienced only once, in 1917, during the brief period between the democratic February Revolution and the Bolshevik October Revolution. With these exceptions, authoritarianism was the rule in Russian governance.

For centuries, Russia was an absolute monarchy, ruled as a paramilitary garrison state to protect against threats internal and external. As George Vernadsky, Yale University's distinguished professor of Russian history, described it: "In the Tsardom of Moscow of the sixteenth and seventeenth centuries we find an entirely new concept of society and its relation to the state. All the classes of the nation, from top to bottom, except the slaves, were bound to the service of the state...."[3] This state, moreover, was ruled by hereditary tsars who held absolute power, issuing decrees which had the force of law. The Russian *ukaz* (decree) has come into English as *ukase* (a decree having force of law).

Internally, Russia's rulers, seeing social unrest and political dissent as threats to their ability to govern a vast empire, did not hesitate to use force to maintain their authority. Externally, they saw Russia surrounded by hostile powers, and they took advantage of any weakness along its periphery to secure its borders and extend its territorial reach.

With power concentrated at the center, the influence of the state on Russian society has been pervasive. Crown, church, and aristocracy were the largest landholders. Many sectors of the economy were controlled or subsidized by the state. Service to the state was the primary duty of both rulers and ruled.

In the Soviet era, the state played an even greater role. Moscow's heavy hand was found in the economy, culture, education, the media, religion, and citizens' private lives—planning, directing, instructing, and stifling initiative in the process. Big Brother—or rather Big Daddy, in a paternalistic society—was everywhere.

Commenting on Russian governance, George F. Kennan writes:

> Forms of government and the habits of governments tend over the long run to reflect the understandings and expectations of their peoples. The Russian people, like a number of other peoples of the Soviet Union, have never known democracy as we understand it. They have experienced next to nothing of the centuries-long development of the discipline of self-government out of which our own political culture has evolved.[4]

The result has been a usually submissive citizenry (at least until 1990), accustomed to—indeed expecting—direction from above, being told what to do and what to think. "It is difficult for us to make decisions," a Russian psychologist told me. "We are so used to being told what to do that we cannot take the initiative and decide for ourselves."

Another centuries-old tradition is a state-sanctioned ideology that serves as a moral guide, determining what is right and wrong. In the tsarist era, the ideology was Russian Orthodoxy, the state religion. In the Soviet period, the Communist party imposed its own standards of cultural, moral, and political behavior. According to the now defunct Article 6 of the Soviet Constitution, the Communist party "determines the general perspectives of the development of society and the course of the domestic and foreign policy."

The revocation of Article 6 in 1990 released a wave of creativity and initiative. Independent organizations and nascent political parties have sprung up, free of government control. Among these are groups devoted to politics, economics, ecology, culture, sports, and other recreational activities as well as charity and voluntary work.

According to Librarian of Congress James Billington, in mid-1990 there were as many as 60,000 of these informal social organizations, publishing some 1,000 journals of independent thought.[5] Many of these publications received official recognition when they were registered by state authorities under a new press law adopted in the summer of 1990. The informal groups and their publications may be found in virtually all cities, where they have successfully challenged the authority of the state and planted the seeds for grass roots democracy.[6]

The contrasts between Russia and America are again apparent. In America state power has been limited and diffused, both within the federal government and between federal and state authorities. Free elections and a multiparty system have ensured representation of the popular will. A government role in culture and the media has been eschewed. Church and state have been separate, and the rights of religious minorities protected. The development of moral and cultural values has been left to private institutions independent of government—the press, churches, universities, and that typically American institution, the private voluntary organization. An economy based on private property and the free market, although at times assisted and regulated by the government, has remained free from state control.

The Bureaucracy

> More than in any other country, officials in Russia considered themselves a superior species, appointed to drive the herds of human cattle. Obedience and patience were required of the cattle, willingness to wait for hours and days for a decision, and acceptance of the decision when given.
> —Hugh Seton-Watson, *The Decline of Imperial Russia*

In this description of Russian officials, the English historian Seton-Watson was writing about nineteenth-century Russia. His words, however, would be equally valid for the Russia of our time, where the tradition of an omnipotent, obstinate, and obstructionist bureaucracy still obtains. Americans who interact with Russia will need to understand this bureaucracy and learn how to deal with it.

A diplomatic colleague of mine who had previously served in Iran and Syria told me that after his posting to Moscow he felt very much at home. As in the Middle East, he said, papers go from desk to desk in the bureaucracy, responsibility is diluted, and decisions are referred to higher-ups. (He might have added that such behavior is not limited to Russia and the Middle East but is also found in most developing countries.)

Before proceeding with joint endeavors, Americans should have the approval of all the government agencies involved, which is easier said than done. Doing business in Russia, explains John Blaney, economics counselor at the American Embassy in Moscow, is "almost like a three-dimensional chess game, where each level has different rules and different pieces, and every once in a while, on any level, all the rules change."[7]

Some officials, to be sure, are creative, decisive, motivated, and could easily hold their own on Wall Street or Madison Avenue. They are exceptions, however, and stand out among all the others. Most bureaucrats whom Americans will meet— "dead souls" they are called in Russian—prefer to follow established practice rather than show initiative and risk errors which might prejudice their careers.

The result is rigidity, incompetence, sloth, conservatism, and a tendency to avoid responsibility by passing the buck to higher-ups. Supervisory officials, moreover, are responsible for the errors of their underlings and can be severely disciplined when mistakes are made. What to do?

As one long-time Russian interpreter advised me, "Americans should understand that many Russian officials they will do business with are incompetent and hold their jobs only because of nepotism, friendships, or party membership. Americans should try in advance to get the names of competent officials and seek them out." This can be done with a little homework—contacting colleagues who have previously negotiated with the officialdom and learning which officials to seek out and which to avoid.

In agriculture alone there were three million officials in 1989—compared with two million farmers in the United States—according to Nikolai Shmelyov, a leading economist. Shmelyov recommended dismissal of most of these officials as a step toward reforming a system that currently cannot feed the people.[8] A comparison of agriculture in the Soviet Union and North America showed that, for the same amount of land, material input, and labor, Soviet farms produced less than half as much as U.S. and Canadian farms in similar climatic areas.[9]

A class apart from other citizens, officials enjoy special privileges according to their rank. These include better housing, access to cars, opportunities to receive bribes, foreign travel and assignments abroad, medical treatment in elite clinics and hospitals, and vacations at comfortable resorts at nominal prices. Their children also receive preferential treatment through admission to select schools and universities as well as appointments to preferred jobs upon graduation.

At the higher levels of the bureaucracy, until the collapse of Communist rule, was the *nomenklatura*, the lifelong tenured positions filled by Communist party appointees on the basis of political reliability. Wielding great power, the nomenklatura had a vested interest in maintaining the status quo and was positioned to block or slow down change. As described by the late Andrei Sakharov, Nobel Peace Laureate and human rights activist:

> This elite has its own life style, its own clearly defined social status—"bosses" and "chiefs"—and its own way of talking and thinking, the *nomenklatura* has in fact an inalienable status, and has recently become hereditary. Thanks to a complex system of covert and overt official privileges, along with contacts, acquaintances, and mutual favors—and also thanks to their high salaries—these people are able to live in much better housing, and to feed and clothe themselves better (often for less money in special "closed stores"...or by means of trips abroad—which under Soviet conditions, constitute the highest award for loyalty).[10]

Whether a new nomenklatura will reemerge in a reformed Russia remains to be seen. But, based on past experience, it is likely that the bureaucracy will continue to wield great power and that many vestiges of privilege will remain.

"We should abandon everything," Mr. Gorbachev writes, "that led to the isolation of socialist countries from the mainstream of world civilization."[11] Yet, much of the deplored isolation is due to the suspicion that generations of Russian officials have had of foreigners. As Shmelyov says, "They have a peasant mentality about...getting too involved and dependent on the outside world."[12]

How should Americans deal with these officials whose approval will be needed for U.S.-Russian joint endeavors? First, they should attempt to open discussions as high in the chain of command as possible. Decisions on U.S.-Russian relations are rarely made at the working level but are usually referred to more senior officials. The higher one starts, the closer one will be to the person who decides. Indeed, when Americans are able to state their case directly to an official with authority, decisions are made more promptly, if not immediately. But that presents another challenge—to determine who has the authority and who decides.

Prepare the groundwork by presenting in advance a paper outlining your proposal. This will give the bureaucracy time to study the offer, check it out with higher officials, and give a more authoritative response. Such a paper will also help to ensure that the proposal is accurately presented as it works its way up through the bureaucracy. To conform with the Russian approach (the concept first, then the details), begin the paper with a general introduction—the background, history, and even philosophy behind the proposal—before proceeding to the particulars.

An initial *nyet* should not be accepted as a definitive response. Russians can change positions when they know more about an initiative and are persuaded that it is in their interest. Keep talking. Negotiations may be lengthy, and decisions slow in coming (see chapter 6, "Negotiating with Russians"). Everything takes longer in Russia and requires patience and perseverance.

The Germans, who have been doing business with Russia for centuries, have learned from experience. "Many American businessmen," says one German banker, "come to Moscow and leave three weeks later completely frustrated. German businessmen are willing to stay six months to make a deal."[13]

One reason why things takes longer is that Russians feel more comfortable with persons they have known for some time. The familiar face is welcome, and repeated visits to Russia may be necessary before confidence and trust are built.

Gift giving is an old Eastern custom. In Slavic lands visitors have been traditionally welcomed with gifts of bread and salt, the staples of life. The tradition of exchanging gifts continues today but the staples of life have changed. Items not available in Russia or in short supply are very much appreciated—and sometimes suggested—by officials. Bribes are illegal, of course, but between a gift and a bribe there is a narrow line which may be difficult to discern. In any event the gift of a VCR, computer, or stereo system will grease the wheels—as well as the palms— of the bureaucracy. Less costly items will also be appreciated— video films, popular records and cassettes, electronic gadgets, clothing, foodstuffs, whiskey, and almost anything not available in Russia. Women will be grateful for cosmetics, costume jew-elry, fancy soaps, and tights or pantyhose. Gift wrapping is not necessary; more important is the sentiment that is conveyed with the giving. Bring a bag of American souvenirs, especially those with a university, company, or city logo. And in a nation of bibliophiles, books are treasured. Particularly welcome are recent publications by well-known authors, but almost anything in English will do, since demand for English-language books far exceeds supply.

Breaking bread breaks barriers. Russians welcome invitations to lunch or dinner where business can be conducted informally and they will not be speaking "on the record." (The working breakfast, however, is alien to Russian culture and is not yet in vogue.) And visitors from abroad may be invited to Russian homes now that the risk in association with foreigners is gone. Favors are appreciated and will be reciprocated.

The greatest favor would be a much-prized invitation to visit the United States, with dollar costs paid by an American host. Russians have an enormous interest in foreign travel and are especially curious about the United States. Until recently, travel was limited to a favored few. Now, it is much easier to obtain a passport and exit visa, but the shortage of hard currency is still a deterrent, as is the limited number of airline seats. Russians can pay rubles to fly to the United States on Aeroflot, the state airline, but "ruble" seats are limited, and flights are sold out far in advance. A U.S.-Soviet air agreement signed in 1990 greatly increased the number of flights between the two countries, but under its terms, until the ruble becomes convertible, only 8.75 percent of the seats on U.S. airliners flying out of the Soviet Union can be purchased in rubles.

Invitations to visit the United States should be reciprocal, a practice Russians will understand. In many cases, they will be prepared to pay the in-country costs of an American visitor to Russia in exchange for an American covering their costs in the United States.

Contacts with the bureaucracy have increased, but many Americans wonder why they seldom see papers on desks in the offices where they are received. This is because many of the higher officials have two offices—one for work and another for receiving visitors.

Corruption

It's easy to steal when seven others are stealing.

—Russian proverb

"Soviet society in its middle levels is becoming a society of thieves," reported George Feifer in 1981, quoting a formerly idealistic Russian friend. "The assumption that 'everybody steals' is erasing the nation's sense of right and wrong."[14]

In recent years corruption and cynicism have spread. In 1981, Russians had to figure out ways to beat the system in order to obtain scarce consumer goods. Now, with much higher prices and a breakdown in distribution, they must do so in order to eat and survive. Those who recall the food deficits and hunger experienced in wartime find this demoralizing in peacetime, especially in a nation with an agricultural heritage.

As in many Eastern societies, what counts is not what you know but whom you know, and often whom you pay off. *Blat* (influence or pull) is a way of life, along with its cousin, nepotism. Officials have been long accustomed to using their positions to help themselves, their families, and friends. But today, for all citizens, corruption is now a requisite for survival in a society of scarcity and inequities.

A discreet gift will bring favorable treatment in stores and offices. Knowing the right person can mean receiving an apartment or gaining admission to a preferred school or university. And a payoff will bring a home repairman.

Home repairs are no simple task in a country where housing is usually owned by local governments and getting a repairman to make a house call is difficult. But as writer Vassily Aksyonov explains, to have home repairs done expeditiously, you simply "...call in a man, whose name always seems to be Nikolai, and for five rubles in cash he takes care of anything that needs taken care of."[15] Nikolai is likely to be a moonlighter—a state employee, using state materials, and working on state time.

The moonlighter's fee has surely risen since Aksyonov left Russia in 1980, but the "Nikolai factor" applies wherever special attention is needed. Some rubles, a gift, or favor to the right person will place a customer at the top of a list to purchase a scarce item or will grease the wheels of the sluggish bureaucracy. Russians do not consider this to be corruption but rather a fact of everyday life.

Bribery and embezzlement have long been common among officials, but under glasnost an epidemic of corruption in high places was exposed and offenders brought to trial after Mr. Gorbachev assumed power in 1985. In one of these trials, Leonid Brezhnev's son-in-law, Yuri Churbanov, received a twelve-year sentence for bribery in the coverup of widespread corruption by the highest Communist officials in Uzbekistan.

In 1990 the regional Party chief of Volgograd and fourteen other local Party leaders there resigned as a result of public outrage over charges that they had helped friends and relatives to get apartments. Volgograd citizens without connections have had to wait up to fifteen years for scarce apartments.[16]

Under the cultural exchange agreement, when the U.S. State Department after years of effort finally obtained Soviet agreement to an exchange of graduate students in the arts, the first student sent to the United States under the new program was the daughter of the official who had agreed to the exchange. And, as one Russian recently put it, bribes used to be given in envelopes, now they are given in cartons (an allusion to the increased size of the bribes as well as runaway inflation). Most disconcerting to Russians is that this type of illicit behavior, long practiced by officials, has now spread throughout the population. As one of Feifer's Russian friends put it, "Everyone knows that to get ahead in the country, it is almost required that you be a liar or a cheater—often a swine."[17]

Corruption, offensive to Americans, is taken for granted in the cultures of many countries and is not unknown in our own. In Russia, however, corruption has become endemic, a necessity for survival in a society that has been unable to provide for the essential needs of its citizens.

The KGB

No matter how good Western intentions, there were at least two sets of problems which constantly created obstacles to good relations with the Soviet Union; the activities of the KGB and the Soviet treatment of its dissidents.
— Robert A. D. Ford, *Our Man in Moscow*

One part of the bureaucracy works very well: the intelligence service, formerly the U.S.S.R. Committee for State Security but better known by its Russian initials, the KGB. Its espionage activities abroad have been an obstacle to improved relations with many countries, as noted above by Robert Ford, Canada's long-time former ambassador to Moscow. KGB activities abroad are well known to Westerners through films and novels as well as news reports. Less well known abroad are its responsibilities for internal security and the collection of information on domestic affairs.

Russia has had a secret police since the sixteenth century when Tsar Ivan the Terrible established his *Oprichnina* to root out political opposition. The name has changed over the centuries and the scope of its activities has expanded greatly, but its essential purpose has not changed. Russian rulers have continued to maintain a secret police to enforce their will and counter domestic opposition. After the attempted coup of August 1991, the KGB was reorganized and given a new name, the Ministry of Security. Many observers believe, however, that it is as formidable as ever.

The KGB was Stalin's personal instrument for carrying out his reign of terror. According to a former KGB officer who is now an official with the Russian Ministry of Security, material in the KGB archives has disclosed that eighteen million people had been "repressed" from 1935 to 1945–about seven million of whom had been shot. These figures, however, do not include deaths in prison and labor camps by means of execution other than shooting. Many historians, moreover, Russian as well as Western, believe that deaths due to the terror were far greater, exceeding even the twenty million Soviet citizens killed in World War II.[18]

Whatever the number, Stalin's abuses were extensive, and there is hardly a family, especially among the more educated, that was not in some way a victim. Today, with the KGB no longer the feared instrument of the past, Russians will not hesitate to tell Americans about their experiences during the terror.

Many of the Russian officials serving abroad, or at home in state agencies that work with foreigners, are KGB officers or have been co-opted by the KGB to report on their foreign contacts. Americans working with Russians will likely encounter such personnel at some point, although they may not be aware of it.

Encounters with KGB officers need not be a cause of concern. KGB personnel are likely to be intelligent—as well as intelligence—officers who demonstrate flexibility, initiative, and confidence in dealing with foreigners. But they will also be collecting and reporting information on the people they meet.

What is the KGB looking for? Of interest are personal foibles and weaknesses that might be used for blackmail at some future time—unusual lifestyles, addictions, sexual preferences, and financial difficulties.

Foreign visitors to Russia are no longer routinely followed, but hotel rooms and telephones may still be bugged and mail monitored. Any suspicious activity can be expected to attract KGB interest. And the KGB has a long memory. Once an item goes into a person's dossier, it may lie dormant for many years, to surface only when an earlier indiscretion has been long forgotten and the individual in question has reached a position of importance.

A warm personal relationship with a Russian, however, can thwart even the KGB. A former American exchange student in Russia relates how he was assigned to share a dormitory room with a Russian student. Entering his room one day, the American found his roommate amorously involved with a female visitor. "Disappear," growled the Russian. The American quickly retreated but stationed himself outside the door and prevented others from entering the room until the liaison had been concluded. In appreciation, the Russian confessed that he had been assigned by the KGB to report on his roommate. "But since you are such a fine fellow," he added, "just stay in your room and study for a few nights, and I'll say in my report that you are a serious scholar and not a CIA spy."

One final word of caution. Visitors to Russia should not say anything in public—or in a place where it might be overheard—that could get a citizen in trouble with the authorities. Never mention to others the names of friends whose actions or views might make difficulties for them. When Russians trust someone, they will open up and tell everything, but they will also expect that person to respect their confidence.

The Law

If all laws perished, the people would live in truth and justice.
—Russian proverb

When Richard Nixon named his Cabinet after winning the presidential election of 1968, a prominent Russian law professor asked me why so many lawyers had been chosen by the new president. Lawyers do not have much prestige in Russia, and Russians are puzzled by the prominence of lawyers in U.S. public life.

In response to the professor's question, I first cited the trite but true textbook response that the United States has a government of laws and not of men. I next mentioned the significance of private property in U.S. law and the importance of the contract, both of which may require lawyers. My third explanation—more meaningful in the Russian context—concerned the concept of compromise, the foundation of democracy. I explained that in U.S. civil disputes, most lawyers settle their cases through negotiation and compromise; and in criminal law, many charges are settled through plea bargaining—a compromise between lawyers for the state and defense. The meaning was not lost on the professor since *kompromiss*, in Russian, has a pejorative meaning and is considered a sign of weakness and a betrayal of the faith.

More important than the law in Russian culture are truth and justice. The search for social justice is a continuing theme in Russian literature, from Tolstoy to Solzhenitsyn. Reflecting their quest for universal harmony, Russian writers have regretted their country's failure to alleviate suffering and eliminate inequities.

"Bolshevism," wrote Nikolai Berdyaev, "showed itself to be much more faithful to certain primordial Russian traditions, to the Russian search for universal social justice...and to the Russian method of government and control by coercion."[19] Berdyaev, a prominent religious writer, left the Soviet Union in 1922 to settle in Paris.

The law in Russia has served to protect the state rather than the individual. Not surprisingly, Russians discount the law's ability to provide the truth and justice they seek. More important than the legalisms of the law has been the consensus of the community.

In the mir the rule of law did not apply. Decisions were made by the village assembly based on what made sense at the time and appeared just and useful for the common good. Crime was not considered by peasants in the abstract, as Nicholas Vakar notes. Stealing wood from the state or a landowner, for example, was against the law but was not considered by peasants to be a crime. But stealing even the smallest object from a fellow villager or from the commune would bring the culprit a severe beating, at the very least, or even mutilation or death. And the horse thief, as in the American West, was one of society's worst enemies. If caught, he was promptly tortured and lynched without trial. The same was true for arsonists in a land where thatched huts burned quickly and an entire village could easily be destroyed by fire.[20]

Rule in Old Russia was by imperial decree, and the tsar's will was not subject to law. As Richard Wortman writes, "The tsarist state, ever insistent on the supremacy of the executive power, has held the judicial system in disdain, and this disdain was shared by the officialdom and the nobility."[21]

Soviet leaders continued this tradition of being above the law. In the 1960s, when they mounted a campaign against foreign-currency speculators, several suspects were arrested and, in accordance with the Soviet penal code, sentenced to long terms of imprisonment. Public opinion, however, whipped up by press reports on the speculators' high lifestyles, demanded the death penalty.

Nikita Khrushchev, Party chief at the time, summoned the Public Prosecutor General and demanded the death sentence. When told that Soviet law did not permit execution for currency speculation, Khrushchev replied, "Who's the boss: we or the law? We are masters over the law; not the law over us—so we have to change the law...." A law was indeed passed, providing the death penalty for speculating in large sums of foreign currency, and the speculators were tried, some for a second time, sentenced to death, and executed.[22]

Russian and Western law have a common ancestry in Roman law. Indeed, in the year 1000, writes Harold Berman, both Russia and the West looked to the canon law of the Church and the

Roman law of the Christian emperors. But, as Berman adds, the Franks converted to Christianity in 486, and Kievan Rus in 988, and this put Russia five hundred years behind the West in the development of its legal system.[23]

Differences between Russian and Western law derive from Byzantium and Russian Orthodoxy. In Byzantium, the emperor had absolute authority over justice, making and unmaking laws, legislating on religious as well as civil matters, and acting as supreme judge of the land. In Byzantium, moreover, church and state were one, and the emperor was presumed to have the obligation to monitor the morals of his people. Russian law, accordingly, has been more intrusive in personal lives.

Russian Orthodoxy, as Berman notes, was "...little concerned with theology, philosophy or dogma in the strict sense...not so dominated by the priesthood, not so political in its interest or in its basic structure." The Orthodox Church and Russian law emphasized, instead, the community, a common sense of brotherhood and togetherness. This has given Russian law

a strong tradition of collective social consciousness which relies for its motivation less on reason than on common faith and common worship, and which finds expression less in legal formality and 'due process' than in more spontaneous and more impulsive responses.[24]

"The West," continues Berman, "has exalted law, with its principles of Reason, Conscience, and Growth; it has fostered the doctrines of the supremacy and completeness of law, its basis in equality, its organic continuity."[25] But this Western legalism and its time-consuming "due process" has been disdained by many of Russia's greatest minds who have looked to personal and administrative relationships rather than to the formality of the law. Moreover, Berman adds, there is a Russian belief that large areas of life remain outside the law,

particularly in...politics and policymaking, where reliance is placed on the nonrational, nonlegal factors of force and violence, on the one hand, and of moral unity and common faith on the other. The personality of rulers still plays a dominant role; personal influence is a crucial factor in impeding the movement for stability of laws."[26]

Attempts in the late nineteenth century to establish a *Rechtsstaat*, a state based on rule of law—Russians still use the German term—were only partially successful. One hundred years later there is again talk of a Russian Rechtsstaat, but progress in achieving it has been slowed by two factors. First, the level of legal consciousness among the people remains low, and, second, the administration of justice must overcome a history of arbitrary application of the law. Following Russian tradition, the judicial system has been subservient to the state. Judges are appointed for ten-year terms by local governments, and a court's decision, particularly in the provinces, may be influenced by a telephone call to the presiding judge from a local official, a practice known as "telephone law."

In civil law, a citizen can generally expect a fair trial, although the interests of the state will be given priority. In criminal law, however, acquittals are rare. In 1988, only 1 percent of all criminal trials resulted in acquittal.[27]

Defense lawyers work under severe handicaps. An accusatory bias exists against defendants, who are presumed to be guilty; otherwise, why would they be on trial?[28] Most judges are believed to form their opinion on guilt or innocence before a trial even begins. A new law now allows the republics to establish jury trials, but trial by jury, according to Russian legal expert Arkady Vaksberg, is opposed by both conservatives and reformers, often on grounds that "the level of legal consciousness of the population" is inadequate.[29]

In criminal law, until new legislation was passed in 1989, lawyers were often unable to obtain access to imprisoned defendants and their case files until the eve of the trial, after the police investigation had been completed. Defense lawyers, as in many European legal systems, do not sit next to defendants during trials and consequently are able to provide only limited counsel. There are no court stenographers and no verbatim trial records to assist lawyers in preparing appeals. Not surprisingly, lawyers do not expect acquittals.

In 1989 there were 27,000 practicing *advokaty* (lawyers) in the entire Soviet Union, and only 1,100 for Moscow's nine million residents—one for every 10,600 Soviet citizens (compared with one for 418 in the United States).[30] Also in contrast to the United States, lawyers have little social status or political influence, no importance in the legal system, and are poorly paid. In public life, until recently, membership in the Communist party was more important than training in law. With the exception of Mr. Gorbachev and Lenin, who both studied law, political leaders have usually been engineers by training. Mr. Yeltsin's education and work experience, for example, is in construction engineering.

In America, law limits power, both public and private. Americans, although they may not always observe the law, respect it and believe that it embodies truth and justice. The judicial system is expected to determine truth and deliver justice.

In Russia, endless exceptions to the law are allowed which permit almost any outcome sought by the courts and the state. As Russian legal scholar Larisa Afanasyeva puts it, "Even when good laws were adopted, there was an enormous gap between what the law said and how it was enforced. And in the gap is the bureaucracy."[31]

Contracts signed in good faith may be subject to social and political interpretation. What value, then, one might ask, has an agreement or contract signed between U.S. and Russian business representatives or partners in cultural and scientific exchanges?

Officials who negotiate such agreements are usually experienced with and understand the nature of a contract. The same cannot always be said, however, for directors of the new cooperatives and private businesses.

When differences arise in implementing a contract, Russian courts and other adjudicating agencies can be expected to favor the Russian side. American signatories to such agreements are advised to consult a lawyer before signing. Russian lawyers will know not only the applicable law but also the psychology of court officials and others who may be involved, a factor which may be more important than the law itself. And their fees, in comparison with those of American lawyers, are low.

One aspect of the law where Russian and Western differences are most striking is individual rights. In the West these rights are based on constitutions and laws which spell out the rights of individuals and the limits of state infringement on those rights. To Russians, rigorous application of the law to defend individuals may appear unduly legalistic. They would rather judge each situation in the light of circumstances and weigh the relative interests of the individual and the community, a contest in which community interests may prevail.

Individual rights, moreover, may clash with the communal ethic. Russians are prejudiced against those who live differently or better than their neighbors. In a culture that values harmony of thought and the communal good, persons who differ from the established order are suspect. *Individualysti* (individualists)— which has a pejorative meaning in Russian—appear opposed to the sense of community as the basis for social good.

"Tolerance was never one of the qualities instilled in people in our political culture," says Tatyana Zaslavskaya, a prominent Russian sociologist. "Such bourgeois notions of tolerance were uprooted, and people were made to believe there was only one truth: 'Those who are not with us are against us.' It will take years, maybe generations to overcome this."[32]

Order and Disorder

[Russia]... this most anarchic of nations.
—Francine du Plessix Gray, *Soviet Women*

Germans are known for *ordnung* (order), and Russians for *nyeporyadok* (disorder). Yet both order and disorder coexist in

Russia, a fact of life to which visitors from the West will have to reconcile themselves.

In Russian literature it is Germans who demonstrate order, discipline, and efficiency. The classic example is Stolz in Ivan Goncharov's novel, *Oblomov*, who is a model man of action, while Oblomov, his Russian opposite, is a man of inaction who spends the first fifty pages of the novel getting out of bed in the morning. Oblomov is a favorite character of Russians, who see something of themselves in his inaction and disorder. It was not by accident that many high officials and diplomats of Tsarist Russia were ethnic Germans from Russia's Baltic territories.

The Russian desire for order arises from the need of her rulers to bring a measure of discipline to an unruly people and marshal their productive potential for the security and well-being of state and society. Disorder derives from the anarchic strain in Russians, their rebellion against regimentation, and their flouting of regulation when they believe they can safely do so.

Westerners who arrive at Moscow's modern Sheremetyevo Airport—built by West Germans—are struck by the confusion, in contrast to the efficiency of West European airports. By Russian standards, however, Sheremetyevo is well run because it is a gateway to the country and was built to serve foreign travelers. The further one travels from Moscow, the greater the airport confusion.

One winter night in 1988 I changed planes in Sverdlovsk, Boris Yeltsin's home town and a Siberian city that was closed to foreigners at the time. In fact, I must have been one of the first Americans in Sverdlovsk since U-2 pilot Gary Powers unexpectedly deplaned there in 1960. A major industrial center with a regional population of more than three million, Sverdlovsk had no Intourist facilities and no special services for foreign travelers. (Sverdlovsk, renamed Yekaterinburg, was not officially opened to foreigners until 1990.)

The Sverdlovsk air terminal recalled scenes of New York's Grand Central Station during rush hour. A huge crowd jammed a concourse the size of a football field. The public address system was barely intelligible. There were no seats and no places to rest except the restrooms, which also had no seats.

When my flight was called, late as usual, there was the customary pushing and shoving at the flight gate, not unlike a rugby scrum. After passengers were finally corralled into a small holding area and left standing, jammed together like sardines, there were further unexplained delays. When a bus eventually disembarked us at the plane's ramp, we were left to wait another half hour in the frigid Siberian night while the plane was being readied. Between flight gate and plane ramp, tickets and identity documents of all passengers had been checked three times. In 1992 in Moscow, I had the same experience on a domestic flight.

Russian governments have had two main tasks, writes Berkeley's Martin Malia—to maintain order internally and wage war externally.[33] Internal order meant keeping the peasants in line, since they were some 90 percent of the population. Without a strong hand, both tsars and commissars believed that the unruly Russians would quickly descend into anarchy.

"Try to understand the regimented way in which we live," a Russian teacher explained to me. "Things here are either yes or no, with no shades of interpretation in between."

There are regulations for everything. Uniformed militia are seen everywhere in the cities, controlling pedestrian as well as motor vehicle traffic and enforcing regulations which often do not make sense. Hingley relates how beachmasters at Black Sea resorts would blow whistles to command sunbathers to turn over at intervals so as to avoid sunburn (a command ignored by the sun-loving Russians).[34] Jaywalking is strictly forbidden, and violators risk being cited by the militia.

What should an American do when stopped by the militia for some minor infringement? My recommendation is to keep talking without raising your voice, admit to your transgression if you are clearly in the wrong, but also explain any extenuating circumstances. You can't beat city hall, in Russia as in America, but the militia can have a heart if appealed to on a personal level, and if their authority is not questioned.

Shoppers will be annoyed by the number of reasons the bureaucracy can find to inconvenience them by closing stores. On certain days stores are closed for *inventar* (inventory), *remont* (repair), and *sanitarny dyen* (cleaning day). And most stores close for one or two hours each day for lunch as well.

Motor vehicles are not allowed to make left turns, unless there is a traffic light with a green arrow. To turn left, drivers must proceed to a designated point where a *razvorot* (U-turn) may be made (very cautiously). It is only a few blocks from Spaso House, the American ambassador's residence in Moscow, to the Ministry of Foreign Affairs, but to get there by car the ambassador must drive more than a mile, making two U-turns along a circuitous route.

Motor vehicles can be ticketed for being dirty. One wintry day in Moscow I was stopped by a militiaman for having a few inches of fresh snow on the hood of my car. My protests that the snow was clean were to no avail.

Returning to Moscow once with my family by rail from the West, I purchased a basket of food in Vienna to sustain us over the thirty-six-hour journey, since there was no dining car on the Soviet leg of the route. At Brest, the Polish-Soviet border crossing, a diligent Soviet agricultural inspector rummaged through our food basket. Spying the bananas, she warned that they could not be brought into the Soviet Union. (Whether this was to protect the Soviet banana crop was not made clear.) "What to do?" I asked. "Eat them," she replied. So my children ate the bananas and brought the peels into the Soviet Union without objection.

Order is also valued because Russians believe it helps to provide a clear view of the future and thus avoids the uncertainty that they so dislike. Communism played on this fear of the unknown by promising everything for the future, but failing to deliver. This penchant for predicting the future and revising the past—rewriting the history books—has given rise to many jokes. According to one *anekdot*, Russians know the future; it's the past they are not sure of.

Despite the many regulations and the many officials to enforce them, Russia appears disorderly to the Westerner. As Custine saw it in 1839, "Every thing is here done by fits and starts, or with exceptions—a capricious system, which too often accords with the irregulated minds of the people...."[35]

Eighty-five years later, Lenin expressed a similar view:

> It is simply the usual Russian intellectual inability to do practical things—inefficiency and lackadaisicalness. First they bustle around, do something, and then think about it, and when nothing comes of it, they run to complain...and want the matter brought up before the Political Bureau.[36]

Each year about 30 percent of the vegetable crop spoils and does not reach the market. In 1990 forty million tons of grain were lost at harvest time, roughly equal to the amount of grain the Soviet Union had to import from the West in that year with its desperately short hard-currency reserves.[37] Plans in industry are fulfilled without regard to cost or quality control. Waste is widespread. Grandiose projects are begun and left unfinished. Wherever people congregate, there is an atmosphere of chaos.

Despite their manifest disorder Russians appreciate the need for order, and many of them who visit the United States are confused by what they regard as the disorder of America. How can there be such abundance without a plan, central control, and a strong leader? How can there be national direction and unity of purpose with so many political parties, religions, and discordant voices? And how can democracy, seen by many Russians as itself a manifestation of disorder, result in such strength and material abundance?

"Paradoxically," as *New York Times* business writer Leonard Silk observes,

> The Communist states, obsessed with maintaining order and control over their economies and people, are in a state of upheaval, while the capitalist democracies—amid the disorder of intense

political competition and uncertainty over swings in the business cycle...and the 'creative destruction' that flows from rapid technological change—are oases of stability.[38]

"Oases of stability" is an apt term to describe capitalist democracies because they are indeed exceptions to the more common pattern of instability and disorder found elsewhere in the world. For Russia—and many other developing countries—disorder is the norm.

School Days, Rule Days

All of us have been formed by the schools we have attended, but Russians more so. Many of the characteristics described in earlier chapters have been reinforced by their system of schooling.

"Authorities in the Soviet state understand very well," writes Canadian child-education specialist Landon Pearson, "that the school is the most important social institution that exists outside the family for shaping the social and moral development of children."[39]

In the 1990s there are debates over education reform, and many changes can be expected, in schools as well as other areas of public life, as political power devolves from the center. Under the reforms of perestroika, writes Harley Balzer of Georgetown University, "...centrifugal tendencies have been the dominant feature of Soviet political life and...authority over schools is increasingly passing into the hands of regional and local governments."[40] But, concludes Balzer, "...given that education is a system and that there is no best variant, the increase in regional diversity is the most hopeful development in the Soviet system in decades."[41]

Diversity is a new phenomenon in Russian education. Until recently, education had a heavy ideological content, was controlled by Moscow, and was uniform throughout the country. And it is to those schools of the past that we must look for an explanation of how schooling has influenced the adult Russians of today.

Schools of the Soviet era had roots in the Russian past. Russian schools traditionally have been more than places to learn readin', writin', and 'rithmetic; they have also been tasked with moral education, the character building that Russians call *vospitaniye* (upbringing). Schools have sought to teach children how to behave and relate to others in society, a Russian version of civic education.

Another tradition, since the nineteenth century, has been uniform curriculum and textbooks, an effort by the center to homogenize its far-flung imperium. As Landon Pearson relates:

It used to be possible...for a youngster to close his geography book in Moscow one morning, fly the long distance to Novosibirsk that afternoon for an extended visit to his grandfather, go to school next day, and find his new class studying the same page he had left the day before.[42]

Other heritages of the past include a Russian preference for the spoken form of communication, which favors oral over written exams, and a dependence on rote replies.

Soviet education continued these traditions, and added some new ones. An extensive system of public schools blanketed the country, eliminated illiteracy, and raised the general level of learning among the populace. Vospitaniye continued in the schools but was manipulated to serve the politics of the Party. Indoctrination of political and social values began in kindergarten and continued through the school years in an effort to form a new "Soviet person," better able to contribute to the building of socialism.

The Soviet theory of education originated in the 1930s with Anton Makarenko, an influential educator who had worked for many years training young criminals and delinquents in correction camps of the secret police. "Makarenko's theory became the official theory of Soviet education," write historians Mikhail

Heller and Aleksandr Nekrich. "The child should be educated as a member of a collective organized along semi-military lines and should be instilled with respect for the authority of the collective and of the person chosen to lead it."[43]

From their earliest years, pupils in Soviet schools were taught to think and act collectively, respect the authority of the teacher, and observe the rules of the classroom. (In Russian, *uchenik* (pupil) is used for primary and secondary schools while *student*, as elsewhere in Europe, is reserved for those in higher education.) "A respectful and, indeed, slightly fearful attitude to adult authority," writes Landon Pearson, "is inculcated into Soviet children from the moment they set foot into an educational establishment. The degree of respect (and fear) increases with the age and status of the older person."[44]

Discipline was strict, and there was little or no discussion in the classroom. For each question by the teacher there was one correct answer, and pupils soon learned that knowing the "right" answer would ensure good grades, which in turn would lead to admission to higher education, a good job after graduation, and the perks that the state offered its educated elites. There were no electives, and teachers taught the required curriculum with little concern for the individual needs of pupils.

Americans who have visited Soviet schools, writes Cathy Young, a Russian who emigrated to the United States in 1980:

> ...tend to find that Soviet schoolchildren, while usually ahead of American students in knowledge of their subjects, are much less likely to be able to think for themselves, and to have their own opinions. Today in the changed climate in the Soviet Union, both educators and students openly complain in newspaper and magazine articles that the Soviet educational system is geared toward producing obedient robots who do what they are told to do and think what they are told to think.[45]

In the first school year all pupils became members of their first collective, the Octobrists. As members of small groups within each classroom, they collectively performed socially use-ful activities such as clean-up work at the school, critiqued their classmates' attitudes toward learning, and heard lectures on Lenin and the Soviet Motherland. In the third year they became Young Pioneers, and the level of group activity and political indoctrination increased. At age fourteen, most joined the *Komsomol* (Young Communist League), the prelude to Party membership. Peer pressure to join, as well as the penalties for failure to do so, proved difficult to resist. The popularity of these organizations, however, declined after 1985, and they were dis-solved in 1991.

The needs of the economy also shaped education, alternating between two conflicting needs of the state. The expanding economy required better-educated workers, which required more years in school. But, as the economy expanded and productivity declined, more workers were needed, which called for reducing the time spent in school and moving graduates more rapidly into the work force. The result was a back and forth of policy changes and reforms between general education designed to prepare for entrance to higher education (universities and colleges) and general education combined with vocational training and pro-ductive labor. That controversy continues in the 1990s.

The system was essentially two-track. Some students com-pleted ten years of general education and went on to higher education. Others ended their general education after eight years and transferred to vocational schools that trained future workers, or to specialized secondary schools that prepared stu-dents for skilled occupations as well as for higher education in specialized industrial fields. Education was compulsory, free of charge, and coeducational. Schooling began at age seven and continued for ten years, five hours a day, six days a week.

In recent years the conflict between general education and vocational training has been temporarily resolved by adding another school year, for a total of eleven, but this was done by starting school one year earlier, at age six. And, in a concession to advocates of vocational training, pupils in all schools have

been required to learn a trade that will qualify them for employ-
ment.

Today, four years of primary education are followed by five of
"incomplete" secondary education. After these nine years, about
half of all pupils complete two more years of general secondary
education in preparation for higher education. The others transfer either to vocational schools or specialized secondary schools.
Parental pressure, however, has increased the demand for higher
education and its rewards, and since the 1970s it has also been
possible for graduates of vocational schools to enter colleges and
universities.

For the gifted and talented there are special schools for math,
science, and the arts. Some schools specialize in foreign languages, producing graduates who are nearly bilingual.

With no formal division between primary school, "incomplete" secondary, and secondary school, pupils in the general
education track remain in the same building with the same
classmates, often in the same homeroom, throughout all eleven
years of school, forging strong bonds of friendship that last
throughout life. Many of the friends and familiar faces with
whom Russians feel so comfortable and secure, are based on
these old school ties.

Applicants to higher schools take oral and written exams at
the end of the ninth and eleventh years as well as entrance
exams given by each institution of higher education. Some 20
percent of the 18-21-year age group are enrolled in higher
schools (compared with more than 50 percent in the United
States). Moreover, in the 1989-1990 academic year, 42 percent
of all higher education students were enrolled in evening or
extension courses rather than studying full-time.[46]

In making application for higher education, rural area
applicants are handicapped because they do not always know
what openings will be available at which institutions. In Russia,
there is no Barron's Guide which lists universities and their
courses of study, and students usually apply to a school near
their homes. The less prestigious higher schools often cannot fill

their quotas, but competition for entrance to the elite institutions is very keen, and it is not unknown for nepotism, influence, and bribery to play a role. There is no gender discrimination in admissions. Indeed, the number of male and female students is about equal. Women, however, predominate in the humanities, medicine, and education, a result more of traditional Russian notions of "female" occupations than overt discrimination.

The broad liberal arts education leading to a B.A. degree, as in the United States, is unknown in Russia. Rather, higher education is narrowly specialized to produce graduates in professions needed by the economy. On applying to a university or higher school, students must choose their major field of study, and that choice may well determine whether they are accepted. For decades, a quota for first-year students in each field of study was determined by future needs of the economy as established by the five-year economic plans. For example, projections for petroleum engineers needed five years hence determined the number of students allowed to enter the five-year study program in petroleum engineering. In recent years, however, higher schools have been given increased flexibility in determining their enrollments.

Freshmen are formed into *gruppi* (groups) within each department. With no electives until the final year or two, students remain in these groups with the same classmates through all their undergraduate years, a continuation of the group bonding that began in primary school.

The length of study for teachers is four years, and for most other students, five years, leading to a diploma. Medical doctors study six years. Upon graduation, students are required to accept a three-year job assignment and work where they are needed.

Graduate study, the *aspirantura*, is three years and leads to the *kandidat nauk* (candidate of sciences) degree, somewhat short of a Western doctorate. Full professors usually have the full doctorate, considered higher than a Western Ph.D., and earned after additional research.

Instruction is largely theoretical and highly specialized. Students listen to lectures and take notes but do not challenge their professors. Indeed, more deference is shown to professors than in the United States, another sign of Russian respect for their elders and those with higher status. Russian students excel in mathematics and science, but the system does not produce well-rounded scientists able to respond to the challenges of technological change they will face in the workplace. Russian universities, moreover, emphasize teaching. Research, for the most part, is the preserve of the various academies of science, which also award academic degrees. The separation of teaching and research is a shortcoming of Russian higher education and a recognized handicap for both students and professors.

Russians who visit the United States are impressed by teacher-student interaction, the encouragement of independent thinking rather than knowing the right answers, the choice of electives, independent study, the self-reliance of American students, and the responsibility they assume for their own education. A vocal minority of educators has been pressing for such changes, but reform efforts have been slowed by a conservative bureaucracy and a teaching profession that resists change. With the republics having achieved independence, the reform movement in education is likely to gather speed.

Student exchange is increasing and provides one of the best ways to understand Russians and how they live and study. Life in Russia, to be sure, is not easy. There are continuing *defitsity* (deficits, or critical shortages), and American students who live on the local economy will share the same shortages. As Rachel Connell, a Wellesley College student on the American Collegiate Consortium (ACC) exchange, reported:

> In four months of living in Moscow, my most rewarding shopping day occurred when I found toilet paper and sugar in the same store. Most of the time it is impossible to find either of these products—finding them together was nothing short of a miracle. I dove into the lines and emerged triumphant, my bag filled.[47]

Student exchange also has other rewards. As Oberlin College student Gregory Rigdon wrote after spending a year in Moscow on the ACC exchange:

> I spent five days in a little village 18 kilometers from where Gorbachev grew up. I went to classes at the local school, went horseback riding with Cossacks, heard the stories of how Germans occupied the village... It was simply an experience that would not have been possible on any other undergraduate exchange. I went there with one of my roommates and saw no foreigners for the duration of our stay. To sum up, before I went to the Soviet Union, I thought I knew the answers. Now I do not even know the questions. I have learned a great deal. I am just beginning to grasp the complexity of this country.[48]

[1]Fyodor Tyutchev, quoted by Billington, *Ikon and Axe*, 320.

[2]Stites, *Revolutionary Dreams*, 76.

[3]George Vernadsky, *The Mongols and Russia* (New Haven: Yale University Press, 1953), 337.

[4]George F. Kennan, "After the Cold War," *New York Times Magazine*, 5 Feb. 1989, 38.

[5]James H. Billington, testimony at hearing on *Soviet Disunion: Creating a Nationalities Policy*, Subcommittee on European Affairs, Committee on Foreign Relations, U.S. Senate, 101st Cong., 2d sess., 1990. S. Hrg. 101-887, 32.

[6]For a partial listing of names, addresses, and telephone numbers of informal organizations in various Soviet cities, see *Neformalniye: A Guide to Independent Organizations and Contacts in the Soviet Union* (Seattle: World Without War Council, 1990).

[7]*New York Times*, 23 Mar. 1991.

[8]Nikolai Shmelyov, quoted by Flora Lewis, *New York Times*, 5 July 1989.

[9]Roy L. Prosterman and Timothy Hanstad, *The Prospects for Individual Peasant Farming in the U.S.S.R.* (Seattle: Rural Development Institute, 1991), 6.

[10]Andrei D. Sakharov, *My Country and the World*, translated by Guy V. Daniels (New York: Alfred A. Knopf, 1975), 25-26.

[11]Mikhail Gorbachev, at Central Committee Plenum (5 February 1990), *Washington Post*, 6 Feb. 1990.

[12]Lewis, *New York Times*, 5 July 1989.

[13]Ferdinand Protzman, "2 German-Soviet Pacts Called Vital First Steps," *New York Times*, 15 June 1989.

[14]George Feifer, "Russian Disorders," *Harper's*, (Feb. 1981), 49-50.

[15]Vassily Aksyonov, *In Search of Melancholy Baby* (New York: Vintage Books, 1989), 77.

[16]*Washington Post*, 6 Mar. 1990.

[17]Feifer, "Russian Disorders," 50.

[18]*RFE\RL Research Report 1*, no. 16 (17 April 1992): 70.

[19]Nikolai Berdyaev, *The Origin of Russian Communism* (Ann Arbor: The University of Michigan Press, 1960), 113.

[20]Nicholas P. Vakar, *The Taproot of Soviet Society* (New York: Harper and Brothers, 1962), 75.

[21]Richard S. Wortman, *The Development of a Russian Legal Consciousness* (Chicago: University of Chicago Press, 1976), 3.

[22]Nikita Khrushchev, quoted by Konstantin M. Simis, *USSR: The Corrupt Society* (New York: Simon and Schuster, 1982), 29-31.

[23]Harold J. Berman, *Justice in the U.S.S.R.* (Cambridge: Harvard University Press, 1963), 191.

[24]Ibid., 222.

[25]Ibid., 269.

[26]Ibid., 270.

[27]*Izvestiya*, 23 May 1989.

[28]For much of the material on Soviet lawyers I am indebted to Robert Rand, *Comrade Lawyer, Inside Soviet Justice in an Era of Reform* (Boulder: Westview Press, 1991).

[29]Arkady Vaksberg, "Meeting Report." Lecture at the Kennan Institute, Washington, D.C., 11 April 1989.

[30]Rand, *Comrade Lawyer*, 57.

[31]*New York Times*, 9 Dec. 1989.

[32]*Washington Post*, 18 Jan. 1990.

[33]Martin Malia, "What Is the Intelligentsia?" In *The Russian Intelligentsia*, edited by Richard Pipes (New York: Columbia University Press, 1961), 7.

[34]Hingley, *Russian Mind*, 207.

[35]Custine, *Empire of Czar*, 496.

[36]V. I. Lenin, *Selected Works* 9 (New York: International Publishers, 1943), 356.

[37]*New York Times*, 20 Aug. 1990.

[38]*New York Times*, 9 June 1989.

[39]Landon Pearson, *Children of Glasnost, Growing Up Soviet* (Seattle: University of Washington Press, 1990), 94.

[40]Harley Balzer, "From Hypercentralization to Diversity, Continuing Efforts to Restructure Soviet Education," *Technology in Society* 13 (1991): 124.

[41]Ibid., 143.

[42]Pearson, *Children of Glasnost*, 93.

[43]Mikhail Heller and Aleksandr M. Nekrich, *Utopia in Power, The History of the Soviet Union from 1917 to the Present*, translated by Phyllis B. Carlos (New York: Summit Books, 1986), 286.

[44]Pearson, *Children of Glasnost*, 111-12.

[45]Cathy Young, *Growing Up in Moscow, Memories of a Soviet Girlhood* (New York: Ticknor and Fields, 1989), 79.

[46]Balzer, "From Hypercentralism to Diversity," 134.

[47]Rachel Connell, *Crossways* 1, Newsletter of the American Collegiate Consortium for East-West Cultural and Academic Exchange, Middlebury, Vermont (Spring 1991): 2.

[48]Gregory Rigdon, *Crossways* 1 (Fall 1990): 7.

5

Personal Encounters

Russians are more emotional, more likely to strike deep friendships, less superficially gregarious. They make great sacrifices for those within their trusted circle, and they expect real sacrifices in return. Their willingness, indeed their eagerness, to engage at a personal level makes private life in Russia both enormously rich and incredibly entangling. Close emotional bonds are part of Russia's enchantment and also its complexity.
—Hedrick Smith, *The New Russians*

The City

The city itself in Russia is an implanted thing, and...the urban man who has created the civilizations of the West is still in the making here. His habitual loneliness, his totally private life, his ignorance of his neighbors, his go-it-alone psychology—these are still in conflict in Russia with an older way of communal existence.
—Inge Morath and Arthur Miller, *In Russia*

First-time visitors to Russia will be struck—literally as well as figuratively—by the large crowds of people they encounter and the ever-present body contact. Russian cities swarm with people.

Forced industrialization moved masses of *muzhiks* (peasants) from the warm and personal environment of their native villages to the cold and impersonal surroundings of large cities. Between 1926 and 1939, the Moscow and Leningrad regions grew by three-and-one-half million each.[1]

There is no real analogy in America, as Morath and Miller point out, although Americans can look back to something similar in their own cities in the days before World War I

> when the cities were filling up with country people who had to learn to be up-to-date—to forget the ideas of mutual help...and to relate themselves to an impersonal administration rather than to officials they knew and to personalities they understood and who understood them.[2]

Most urban residents are only two or three generations removed from their ancestral villages and peasant traditions. As Hingley describes them, "...even in the towns—in Moscow or Tula, say—a Russian crowd seems to react in a more peasant-like manner, however defined, than would be the case in Rome, Munich or Pittsburgh."[3] The cities became "ruralized," writes Richard Stites, "...imbued with peasant values—at home, on the streets, and at work. Urban civilization did not efface rural mentalities; rather, the opposite occurred."[4]

Despite the dislocations caused by their move from village to city, Russians regard city life as infinitely better than life in the village. In the city there are new opportunities, not only for work but also for education, culture, and recreation. Housing and municipal services, however, have not kept pace with the large influx of new residents.

Most city dwellers live in small apartments in large multistoried buildings rather than in detached houses. Due to the housing shortage, some 15 to 18 percent of the urban population in 1989 was still living in communal apartments—one family occupying one or two rooms while sharing a kitchen and bathroom with as many as five other families.[5] The need to find relief from indoor crowding is one reason why so many Russians are on the streets. The constant search for scarce items is another, and explains why practically everyone carries shopping bags or briefcases.

With goods and services always in short supply, Russians spend an inordinate amount of time shopping for food, clothing, consumer products, and other scarce items that sell out quickly. If a shopper is not there when something goes on sale, an opportunity is lost and may not come again for some time.

Citizens wait in line to purchase scarce items of poor quality that would be rejected by most people in the West. Items in short supply or simply not available in recent years include soap, razor blades, tobacco, toothpaste, toilet paper, good shoes, and food staples such as meat, cheese, vegetables, fruit, and good tea. Until the late 1920s, Russia was an exporter of wheat, rye, barley, and oats. Now, it must import grain and other agricultural commodities and pay for them with foreign currency.

In most stores, customers stand in line three times to make one purchase—first to learn what is for sale and how much it costs, then to pay a cashier, and finally to present the cash receipt to a salesperson and pick up the purchase.

Shortages and unmet demands for basic necessities of life can make Russians very aggressive about trying to acquire things they need but do not have, and they are not bashful about making such requests to Americans who may be put off by their persistence. A "no" is never accepted by Russians as an initial response. Believing that every response can be manipulated and changed, they will repeat their requests over and over again, adding a new twist each time.

Requests to Americans may be for medicines not available in Russia, scholarships at American universities, books or laboratory equipment required for research, and assistance in emigrating. Visitors will need to be patient in rebuffing requests that they cannot or do not wish to fill. They should also not make promises they cannot keep or agree to miracles they cannot perform.

One type of request which Americans can easily fill is to help Russians establish contact with professional counterparts in the United States. Russians will seek names and addresses of persons or organizations in their profession or in fields in which they have a personal interest. The intent is merely to establish contact and exchange information with the outside world, which was difficult to do until recently.

Others may wish to locate relatives in the United States. One Russian I met in the middle of Siberia, whose Texas-born father had emigrated to the Soviet Union during the depression, had been trying for years, without success, through both U.S. and Soviet government channels, to find his long-lost American relatives. On my return home, I was able to locate several of his family members who had been trying for years to locate their Russian cousin. For that Russian, I was indeed a miracle maker.

Large crowds of people make municipal authorities apprehensive, and their response is crowd control. Uniformed police, *militsiya* ("police" was considered a bourgeois term), are omnipresent in Russian cities. At sports events and other activities which attract large crowds, long convoys of militia trucks are parked nearby in case a crowd gets unruly or out of control, as occasionally occurs. In 1982 at a soccer match in Moscow's Luzhniki Stadium some 340 fans were crushed to death by a surging crowd.[6] And more than 500 people were suffocated or trampled to death on Moscow streets in 1953 when Stalin's body lay in state.[7] It is prudent to stay on the fringes of large crowds to avoid being swept away and trampled.

Russians do not always queue up naturally as do Americans and Britons. Rather than line up and patiently await their turn, Russians will at times storm buildings and box offices—pushing, shoving, and elbowing—determined to gain access or obtain their share before whatever they seek is gone. At airports, even when all passengers are ticketed and have reservations, Russians will throng around the flight gate and plane ramp, anxious lest they not be boarded. To avoid the crush, foreign travelers are usually boarded first.

At popular concerts and sports events, persons without tickets will storm the gate in an attempt to gain admission. Such storming is done not only by the *narod* (common people) but also by the intelligentsia. I witnessed one such Sturm und Drang in 1969 when music students stormed the entrance to the Moscow Conservatory Great Hall, seeking admission to a performance of Bach's *Passion According to St. John* by a visiting West German ensemble. Bach was rarely performed in Russia in those years, and the hall had been sold out far in advance to music lovers with connections.

Masses of people and a chronic scarcity of goods and services combine to make Russians appear brusque, demanding, and insistent—a feature of everyday life.

Friends and Familiar Faces

A person without friends is like a tree without roots.

—Russian proverb

Sol Hurok, the legendary American impresario who pioneered U.S. tours by Soviet dance and music groups, would visit the Soviet Union periodically to audition performing artists and select those he would sign for U.S. appearances. Traveling alone, Hurok would negotiate and sign contracts for extensive U.S. coast-to-coast tours by such large ensembles as the Bolshoi Ballet and Moscow Philharmonic.

On one such trip in 1969, when Hurok was eighty years old, I asked him how he could sign contracts for such large and costly undertakings without lawyers and others to advise him. "I have been coming here for many years and doing business with the Russians," he replied. "I simply write out a contract by hand on a piece of paper, and we both sign it. They know and trust me."

It may indeed take years to establish good working relations with Russians, but once they know and trust someone, much can be accomplished, and without hassle. This also explains the long and successful record of American businessman

Armand Hammer in trading with the Soviets. Hammer had known Lenin, and his dining and dealing with Russians began in 1921.

A different experience is reported by another American, who met in 1990 with a group of Russians from various parts of the country to help them form a national coalition in support of democracy. Assembled in the room were persons with a common purpose and a shared commitment to democracy. Yet, in their first meeting it soon became apparent that their loyalties were to their local organizations, each with its own parochial interests, and not to the national coalition and platform they hoped to forge. Suspicious of each other, they were reluctant to speak up in public. They also did not trust the interpreter, a Russian whom the American had brought with him. Many more meetings were required before the American—talking with the participants individually and in small groups and eating, drinking, and socializing with them—was able to overcome their initial distrust not only of him but of their fellow Russians as well, and eventually help them to forge a viable coalition.

Russians rely on a close network of family, friends, and co-workers as protection against the risks and unpredictability of daily life. In the village commune, Russians felt safe and secure in the company of family and neighbors. Today, in the city, they continue to value familiar faces and mistrust those they do not know. Americans who know a Russian from a previous encounter will have a big advantage. First-time travelers to Russia are advised to ask friends, who already know the persons they will be meeting, to put in a good word for them in advance of their visits.

Despite its vast size, Russia is run on the basis of personal connections. In the workplace and in private life, Russians depend on persons they know—friends who owe them favors, former classmates, and others whom they trust. The bureaucracy is not expected to respond equitably to a citizen's request. Instead, Russians will call friends and ask for their help.

The friendship network also extends to the business world. Business enterprises, constantly short of essential parts and materials, use middlemen called *tolkachi* (go-getters), whose job it is to call or visit tolkachi whom they know at other firms, in search of a deal or trade for the much-needed items. Without such middlemen, production would grind to a halt.

The contrast with America in this regard has been noted by writer Vassily Aksyonov, who now lives in the United States:

> For us, capitalism is modern technology, efficient service, and sound fiscal policy, whereas socialism is outdated technology, rudeness, and primary market relations of the "you scratch my back, I'll scratch yours" variety; favor for favor, commodity for commodity, commodity for favor, favor for commodity. Anything to get by.[8]

Americans who want something from their government will approach the responsible official, state their case, and assume that law and logic will prevail. Russians in the same situation, mistrustful of the state and its laws, will approach friends and acquaintances and ask them to put in a good word with the official who will decide. In Moscow, when Russians need American support on some matter, they will request friends who know someone in the American Embassy to intercede on their behalf with the responsible diplomat. Today, they are also likely to telephone friends in the United States.

The process is two-way, and those who do favors for Russians can expect favors in return. I once offered some friendly advice to a newly arrived Soviet cultural attaché in Washington on how to get things done in America. He returned the favor many times over, smoothing my way through the Soviet bureaucratic maze as we developed a mutually advantageous professional relationship. I was pleased to consider him a friend.

For most Americans, anyone who is not an enemy seems to be a friend. An American can become acquainted with a complete stranger and in the next breath will describe that person as a friend. American friendships, however, are compartmentalized, often centering around colleagues in an office, neighbors in a residential community, or participants in recreational activities. This reflects the American reluctance to get too deeply involved with the personal problems of others. A friend in need may be a friend indeed, but an American is more likely to refer a needy friend to a professional for help rather than become involved in the friend's personal troubles.

Not so with Russians for whom friendship is all encompassing and connotes a special relationship. Dancer Mikhail Baryshnikov, when asked about the difference between Russian and American friendships, replied:

> In Russia, because the society has been so closed, you're sharing your inside with your friends. Your views on society. Political points of view. It's a small circle of people whom you trust. And you get so attached. Talking with friends becomes your second nature. A need. Like, at 4 o'clock in the morning, without a phone call, your friend can come to your house, and you're up and putting the teapot on. That kind of friendship.[9]

The Russian language has different words for friend (*drug*, pronounced droog) and acquaintance (*znakomy*), and these words should not be misused. A drug is more like a "bosom buddy," someone to trust, confide in, and treat like a member of the family. Such friendships are not made easily or quickly. They take time to develop, but when they do, a Russian friendship will embrace the entire person. Russians will ask friends for time and favors that most Americans would regard as impositions.

Friendship with a Russian is not to be treated lightly. One American describes it as smothering, and some will find that it is more than they can handle. As one Russian explained to me, "Between Russian friends, what's theirs is yours and what's yours is theirs, especially if it's in the refrigerator."

Americans tend to be informal in their speech—candid, direct, and without the rituals, polite forms, and indirect language common to many other cultures. Russians welcome and appreciate such informal talk but usually only after a certain stage in the relationship has been reached.

Addressing an American used to present a dilemma for Russians. Their language has equivalents for "Mr." (*Gospodin*) and "Mrs." (*Gospozha*), but until recently these were considered relics of the prerevolutionary past and were not in common use. Now, with the demise of communism, Russians again are using these terms of address.

The preferred form of address among Russians, and the one likely to be used in the initial stage of a relationship, is the first name and patronymic (father's name). For example, Boris N. Yeltsin, whose father was Nikolai, is addressed as Boris Nikolayevich (Boris, son of Nicholas). Similarly, a woman named Mariya whose father was Fyodor (Theodore) would be Mariya Fyodorovna (with the feminine ending *a*). Use of the patronymic does not signify friendship but is less formal than "Mr." or "Ms."

With the friendship stage comes the use of the first name by itself, a practice becoming more common between Russians and Americans as relations between the two countries improve. Russians, like Americans, have a need to be liked by others, particularly by foreigners. But first-name usage with a foreigner does not necessarily indicate that the friendship stage has been reached, as it would with another Russian. It does signify, however, the next stage in a developing friendship.

Like many European languages, Russian has two forms of "you." The more formal *vy* is used between strangers, acquaintances, and in addressing people of higher position. The informal *ty*, akin to the old English *thou* and the French *tu*, is reserved for friends, family members, and children and is used in talking down to someone and in addressing animals.

Which of these forms should Americans use in addressing Russians? That will depend on the state of the relationship, and it may differ in each case. When in doubt, let the Russians decide and follow their lead.

At Home

> At home do as you wish, but in public as you are told.
> —Russian proverb

Russians live two separate and distinct lives—one at work and the other at home. At work, they can be brusque and discourteous, and they watch what they say. At home, within the intimate circle of family and friends, they feel secure and are relaxed, warm and hospitable, sharing and caring, and they speak their own minds.

As Morath and Miller describe it:

> There is still a homeliness about many Russians that has the scent of the country in it, a capacity for welcoming strangers with open, unabashed curiosity, a willingness to show feeling, and above all a carelessness about the passing of time.[10]

When asked what Russians were thinking during the many decades of political repression, legal scholar Nina Belyaeva explained,

> People did not connect themselves with the power of the state. On the one hand, they seemed from outside not to care, so they seemed submissive. But inside, they said, "Inside, I am me. They can't touch me. When I'm in my kitchen with my friends, I am free."[11]

The kitchen is the center of social life, and Americans should not pass up an opportunity to get into those kitchens and see Russians at home. There is no better way to get to know Russians than over food and drink, or merely sitting around a kitchen table sipping tea.

"The secret of social life in Russia," says Stites, "is conviviality around a table, drinking, telling jokes, laughing. When you get to that point, the battle is half won."[12]

Hospitality is spontaneous, intrinsic to the culture. Russians will share what they have and make their guests feel at home.

Dinner may be served in the kitchen or in a parlor that doubles as a bedroom. The dishes may not match and the table service will be very informal, but the visitor will be made to feel welcome and at home. Food will be tasty, and guests will wonder how the many delicacies were acquired in an economy of scarcity and how many hours the hostess had to stand in line to purchase them. As in most European countries, the hot meal is usually taken in the middle of the day, and the evening meal is more like a supper. However, with food shortages the old rules no longer apply, and hosts will serve whatever they are able to find and afford. A meal always begins with wishing others at the table *priyatnovo appetita*, an equivalent of the French *bon appetit*.

Friends and relatives will drop in unexpectedly and join the table. Spirits will flow and the talk will be lively and natural. Conversation is a very important part of social life, and over food and drink Russians open up and reveal their innermost thoughts.

Describing conversations with Russians, British scholar Geoffrey Hosking writes: "...the exchange and exploration of ideas proceeds with utter spontaneity and at the same time concentration. In my experience, the art of conversation is pursued in Moscow at a higher level than anywhere else in the world."[13]

Guests should observe an old custom and bring a gift. Be cautious, however, about expressing admiration for an object in a Russian home. In a spontaneous gesture of hospitality, the host may present the admired object to the guest. Amateur entertainment is popular at social events, and guests should be prepared to sing, recite poetry, or otherwise perform.

Russians welcome inquiries about family and children, and they will be interested in learning about a visitor's family. This interest is genuine and should not be seen as merely making small talk. Family and children are still important in Russian life although society's current ills—overcrowded housing, the lack of privacy, crime, alcoholism, and divorce—have taken their toll. In cities, families with one child are the norm, and I was always surprised when Russians expressed admiration when learning that I was the father of three.

How Americans live is also of great interest. Bring photos of family, home, and recreational activities, which will all be of interest. Russians are curious about the lifestyles of Americans in professions and occupations similar to their own, and they will not hesitate to inquire about a visitor's salary or the cost of a home or car. When a celebrated Soviet writer once visited my home in the Washington suburbs, I expected our talk to be about life and literature. Instead, the world-renowned author requested a tour of the house and was full of questions about the heating, air conditioning, and insulation, and about how much everything cost and whether the house was my year-round home or my weekend *dacha*.

Handshaking is common practice, both on arrival and taking leave, and women should not be surprised if their hands are kissed as well as shaken. Shaking hands over a threshold, however, is an omen of bad luck and should never be done. And if you bring flowers, odd numbers only, please. An even number of flowers is considered unlucky. Old superstitions survive.

Once over the threshold and into the home, you will likely encounter a cloud of smoke. The antismoking campaign has not yet reached Russia, and people are literally smoking themselves to death. In a small apartment or office with windows closed tight in winter, the smoke can be oppressive for nonsmokers.

The Toast

Visitors should be prepared to raise their glasses in a toast. Toasting in Russia is serious business, and in the Georgian republic it is an art form.

Toasts are usually given at the beginning of the meal when vodka is drunk with the first course, or at the end of the meal with the wine or champagne that is served with dessert, and often throughout the meal as well. Hosts toast first, and the ranking guest is expected to follow with a return toast. With each toast, glasses are clinked with those of other guests while looking at each guest directly and making eye contact. The person being toasted also drinks.

In contrast to the laconic American "cheers" or "bottoms up," a toast in Russia is a short speech. To begin, there are the obligatory thanks to the hosts for their hospitality. This may be followed by references to the purpose of the visit, to international cooperation, peace and friendship, and the better world we hope to leave to our children as a result of our cooperation. Be poetic and dramatic, and let your "American soul" show. Russians appreciate a show of emotion and imagination. Don't hesitate to exaggerate, make the most of your toast. Humor may also be used but the substance of the toast should be serious. Russians will judge a toast as an indication of the seriousness of a visitor's purpose. Prudent travelers will have a few toasts prepared in advance—they will surely be needed.

In Georgia, toasting is continuous throughout the meal, and a guest's glass is never left empty. Eating, drinking, and hospitality are a way of life in Georgia, and guests should be prepared for meals that last several hours. Once, when I was in Georgia as the leader of an American delegation, my hosts had the courtesy to ask in advance whether I preferred a three- or four-hour dinner. I opted for the three-hour "short" dinner, which actually lasted five hours—with continuous eating, drinking, animated conversation, music, singing, and endless toasts. *Omnia pro patria.*

Mir i druzhba (peace and friendship) is a toast—as well as slogan—that Americans will often hear in Russia; so often, in fact, that it begins to sound more and more like the political catchphrase that it has been throughout the Communist world.

Of the misuse of the word *peace,* Vaclav Havel, the Czech playwright who became his country's democratically elected president in 1990, writes:

For forty years now I have read it on the front of every building and in every shop window in my country. For forty years, an allergy to that beautiful word has been engendered in me as in every one of my fellow citizens because I know what the word has meant here for the past forty years: ever mightier armies ostensibly to defend peace.[14]

Political slogans aside, the Russian yearning for peace and friendship should not be seen merely as an attempt to delude the West but as a reflection of their traditional yearning for harmony, cooperation, and community. Russians have good reason to want peace and friendship with other countries, although that has not prevented Soviet leaders from using armed force when they have believed it necessary—in Hungary in 1956, Czechoslovakia in 1968, Afghanistan in 1979, and in their own country as well.

World War II with its death and devastation is a part of every citizen's life, experienced either directly or through older family members. More than twenty million Soviet citizens died in the war, and much of European Russia was overrun by German armies before their advance was halted and reversed at Stalingrad. Leningrad was besieged for nine hundred days, and more than a million of its people died there of hunger alone, more than ten times the deaths at Hiroshima. The Great Patriotic War, as the Russians call it, was truly one of the epic events of Russian history which threatened the very existence of the state. More recently, another generation has known war, in Afghanistan.

Do Russians fear a war with the United States? Some of them still do since America is the only country with the military might to vanquish them. Russians, moreover, have a very high respect for American technology, military as well as civilian. When Russians toast "peace and friendship" with Americans, they really mean it.

Alcohol, the Other "ism"

More people are drowned in a glass than in the ocean.
—Russian proverb

To all other "isms" that help to understand Russians, alcoholism must unfortunately be added. For Karl Marx, religion was the opiate of the people. For Russians, the opiate has been alcohol. The Russian affinity for alcohol was described by Custine in 1839:

> The greatest pleasure of these people is drunkenness; in other words, forgetfulness. Unfortunate beings! they must dream, if they would be happy. As proof of the good temper of the Russians, when the mugics [*muzhiks*] get tipsy, these men, brutalized as they are, become softened, instead of infuriated. Unlike the drunkards of our country, who quarrel and fight, they weep and embrace each other. Curious and interesting nation![15]

In our time, the distinguished Russian novelist and literary critic, Andrei Sinyavsky, describes drunkenness as

> our *idee fixe*. The Russian people drink not from need and not from grief, but from an age-old requirement for the miraculous and the extraordinary—drink, if you will, mystically, striving to transport the soul beyond earth's gravity and return it to its sacred noncorporeal state. Vodka is the Russian muzhik's White Magic; he decidedly prefers it to Black Magic—the female.[16]

Per capita consumption of alcohol in Russia and the United States is not very different. Americans, however, drink more wine and beer, Russians more hard liquor, mainly vodka and cognac.

Vodka is described by Hedrick Smith as "one of the indispensable lubricants and escape mechanisms of Russian life.... Russians drink to blot out the tedium of life, to warm themselves from the chilling winters, and they eagerly embrace the escapism it offers."[17]

To take the measure of a man, Russians will want to drink with him, and the drinking will be serious. Americans should not attempt to match their hosts in drinking. This is one competition that Russians should be allowed to win, as they inevitably will.

Vodka is drunk straight, ice-cold in small glasses in one "bottoms-up" gulp. At meals it is served with the *zakuski*, the tasty Russian cold meats, fish, fresh and pickled vegetables, and caviar (when available and affordable). (Guests should bear in mind that the zakuski are only the first course and that several other courses will follow.) With each round of vodka there will be a toast, and the drinking and toasting will continue until the bottle—or bottles—are empty.

What should an American do when confronted with vodka and the obligatory toasts at a dinner where the visitor is guest of honor? If the guest knows when to stop, then by all means, he or she should drink and enjoy it. Guests who fear they will not know their limit can abstain, pleading doctor's orders or religious reasons. Or they can down their first drink and slowly nurse subsequent rounds through the evening.

There are no bars in Russia except those for persons with hard currency, and citizens wishing to drink hard liquor in public must go to a restaurant that serves alcohol. Russians prefer to drink while seated, and the stand-up cocktail party, a Western innovation, is consequently alien. Anyone invited to a Russian home should expect to be seated, to be fed a substantial repast, and to drink during the meal. When invited to an American home, Russians will expect more than chips or cheese and crackers.

A night on the town usually consists of an evening with friends at a restaurant—eating, drinking, and dancing for several hours to very loud pop music. The eating will also be serious. Russians recall the difficult days during and after World War II when food was scarce, and they relish a good meal. Toward the end of the evening there will likely be a bloody brawl among the more serious drinkers, which ends only when the militia arrives.

"Demon vodka," as the Russians call it, is the national vice. Excessive vodka consumption is a major cause of absenteeism, low productivity, crime, traffic accidents, wife beating, divorce and other family problems, birth defects, and a declining longevity.

With the economic, social, and physical ills that it causes, it was not surprising that the first published decree after Mr. Gorbachev took office in 1985 signaled a state campaign against alcohol. The intent was to limit consumption, but the immediate result was a sugar shortage, because Russians purchased more sugar to increase their production of home brew. Consumption of products with alcohol content—industrial alcohol, jet fuel, insecticide, perfume, shoe polish, and toothpaste—also increased, thus creating additional shortages. According to official Soviet sources, more than 10,000 citizens died from these alcohol substitutes in 1987 and more than 11,000 in 1988.[18] The antialcohol campaign also resulted in a 10 to 20 percent reduction in tax revenues.[19] An admitted failure, it was scrapped after three years.

Vodka is a basic ingredient of Russian life and will not be eliminated. During the height of the antialcohol campaign, I attended several official lunches where wine was the strongest drink served, but vodka bottles were passed under the table among the thirsty guests, in a reminder of our own Prohibition days.

Vodka does have one virtue. While it can produce a hangover when drunk to excess, it seldom causes headache or nausea. And with zakuski, in moderation, it is the ideal drink.

Vranyo, the Russian Fib

Yes, the Russian is incapable of telling downright lies; but seems equally incapable of telling the truth. The intermediate phenomenon for which he feels the utmost love and tenderness resembles neither truth nor lozh [lie]. It is vranyo. Like our native aspen, it pops up uninvited everywhere, choking other varieties; like the aspen it is no use for firewood or carpentry; and, again like the aspen, it is sometimes beautiful.

—Leonid Andreyev, *Pan-Russian Vranyo*[20]

Russians can fudge the facts, a national characteristic called *vranyo* (with the accent on the second syllable). Dictionaries translate *vranyo* as "lies, fibs, nonsense, idle talk, twaddle," but like many Russian terms, it is really untranslatable. Americans might call it "tall talk" or "white lies," but "fib" perhaps comes closest because vranyo, as Russian writer Leonid Andreyev noted, is somewhere between the truth and a lie. Vranyo is indeed an art form, perhaps beautiful to Russians but annoying to Americans and others who value the unvarnished truth.

In its most common form today, vranyo is an inability to face the facts, particularly when the facts do not reflect favorably on Russia. Intourist guides are masters of vranyo, as are Russians who represent their country abroad. When ideology or politics dictate a particular position, they are likely to evade, twist, or misstate facts in order to put the best possible spin on a potentially embarrassing situation.

Russians, however, do not consider vranyo to be dishonest, nor should Americans. As Dostoyevsky wrote:

> Among our Russian intellectual classes the very existence of a nonliar is an impossibility, the reason being that in Russia even honest men can lie.... I am convinced that in other nations, for the great majority, it is only scoundrels who lie; they lie for practical advantage, that is, with directly criminal aims.[21]

And, as Dostoyevsky might have put it, if vranyo is not a crime, it should not be punished.

When using vranyo, Russians know that they are fibbing and expect that their acquaintances will also know. But it is considered bad manners to directly challenge the fibber, although it can be done with tact. As British scholar Ronald Hingley advises, the victim of vranyo should "...convey subtly, almost telepathically, that he is aware of what is going on, that he appreciates the performance and does not despise his Russian host simply because the conditions of the latter's office obliged him to put it on."[22]

This advice was put to good use in Moscow once when I was a victim of vranyo. At a lunch given by the American ambassador, all the Russian guests had arrived on time but one, and he had called me the day before to confirm his attendance. After waiting thirty minutes, the ambassador asked me to call our tardy guest and inquire whether we could expect him. An unknown voice took my call and told me that our guest had just suffered a heart attack and could not attend the lunch. Surmising that the illness was diplomatic and that our guest had been instructed by higher-ups not to attend, I called again the next day and our delinquent guest himself answered the phone. After expressing my regrets about his failure to show, I congratulated him on his speedy recovery and wished him continued good health.

On another occasion I had signed a contract with the U.S.S.R. State Concert Agency naming the cities to be visited by an American symphony orchestra touring under the cultural exchange program. One week before the start of the tour, the concert agency informed me that a city had to be dropped because the roof of the hall there, the local opera house, had just caved in. Apparently, someone in the city Party apparatus did not want an American orchestra to perform there, and the roof of the venerable old opera house was the excuse for the vranyo.

Vranyo can also be used at high levels of government. In August 1991 during the attempted coup, Westerners wondered why so many apparently healthy Russian leaders, including Mr. Gorbachev, were said to be ill and unavailable, only to surface in a few days looking quite healthy.

Related to vranyo is *pokazukha*, the tradition of staging something "for show," especially for high officials and visiting foreign dignitaries. The classic example is the Potemkin village, named after one of Empress Catherine the Great's favorites who, according to legend, constructed false village facades along the empress's travel route to show Catherine how well her people were living. A more recent example was the staged opening of the Baikal-Amur Railway in 1984, the target year for its completion, although the huge project was far from finished at the time.

If Russians are compelled by tradition to show only the best, Americans seem obliged to show the worst. As one Russian reported after visiting the United States, everywhere he went his American hosts showed him what was wrong, but also what was being done to correct it. By showing what is wrong, Americans are reflecting their optimism about being able to change things for the better. Russians, by showing the best, are revealing their embarrassment about shortcomings in their society and their inability to deal with them openly.

At times Russians may say something that an American finds patently wrong or unacceptable. Some Americans, preferring to avoid a confrontation, will choose to let it pass. But remaining silent in such a situation may create an impression of acquiescence that would be misleading. Depending on the importance of the issue under discussion, it may be preferable to point out the error even if it should lead to controversy. Russians respect persons who are candid and straightforward. If your facts are true, Russians will not be offended by being corrected. They will also not hesitate to correct an American, and their criticism should be accepted in the same spirit. This is a trait Russians and Americans share.

Nyekulturny

Many an American has confidently entered a Russian theater or restaurant, outercoat hanging over the arm as in the United States, only to be stopped by an usher or waiter and told to first check the coat.

Coats and other outerwear must be checked on entering office buildings, theaters, concert halls, restaurants, museums, and other public buildings. In the lobbies of these buildings visitors will find a *garderob* (cloakroom) staffed by one or more of those ubiquitous Russian grandmothers. The checking procedure is efficient and dependable, and tipping is not customary. Since people must bundle up in cold weather, the mandatory checking of outergarments makes good sense.

Everyday life is full of dos and don'ts, reflecting the state's efforts to impose standards of behavior on a newly urbanized citizenry only recently removed from their ancestral villages. There is a right way and a wrong way to do almost everything. The wrong way is termed *nyekulturny* (uncultured, or bad manners), and a foreign visitor's behavior will be judged by the same standards.

Wearing coats in public buildings is nyekulturny (though Russians see nothing wrong in strolling through hotel corridors clad only in pajamas or bathrobes as if the hotel were a large communal apartment). Also nyekulturny are standing with hands in pants pockets, sprawling in chairs, placing feet on tables, crossing legs while seated so as to show the sole of a shoe, sitting with legs spread wide, crossing arms behind the head, draping an arm over the back of a chair, and merely lounging, all of which Americans are wont to do. An American student recalls being berated in Moscow for lounging on the steps of a public building as he might have done back home. People are expected to behave in public with a degree of decorum. (These are not exclusively Russian attitudes. Disdain for such behavior may be found in other European countries as well.)

Many other liberties that Americans take for granted are also nyekulturny. Students do not eat, drink, or chew gum during class. Eating lunch on park lawns in the city is unacceptable. In the evening, theater patrons are expected to dress appropriately for the opera, theater, and symphony. Immodest dress, whistling on the street, and public displays of affection are also taboo in a traditional and conservative society. One American ambassador, a dapper dresser, drew critical comment when he called on a high Soviet official wearing a pastel shirt with a white collar. In a conservative society, that too was nyekulturny.

Telling Russians that you have to go to the restroom is also nyekulturny. Instead, simply excuse yourself; they'll know where you are going.

Russian performers, public speakers, and others on stage will join their audiences in applause, a move that puzzles Americans. They are, however, not applauding their own performances but are expressing approval and appreciation of the spectators and the response to their performances.

And I have had to explain to high-ranking American officials that whistling in a concert hall after a performance is not a sign of approval, as in the United States, but is a sign of disapproval in Russia (and elsewhere in Europe).

Time and Patience

Punctuality has been exceedingly difficult to instill into a population unused to regular hours...
—Margaret Mead, *Soviet Attitudes toward Authority*

Time is money to Americans, and punctuality a virtue. Meetings are expected to start on time, and work under pressure of the clock is a challenge routinely accepted. To Russians, with their agricultural heritage, time is like the seasons—a time for sowing and a time for reaping, and a time for doing little in between.

Seychas budyit (right away it will be [done]) is an expression heard often in Russia from waiters in restaurants, clerks in stores, and officials in offices. Be assured, however, that whatever has been requested will not be done right away but will more likely take some time.

Communism reinforced the native Russian disrespect for time because workers could not be fired and there was no incentive to do things on time. Moreover, in a country where time is not a vital commodity, people become more sanguine about accepting delays. When something very important must be done, it will be done, and time and cost will not be obstacles. But time for Russians is not an economic commodity to be measured in rubles or dollars.

Being on time is consequently alien. Russians are notoriously not on time, and they think nothing of arriving long after the appointed hour, which is not considered as being late. (Concerts and theater performances do however start on time, and latecomers will not be seated until the first intermission.) But when Russians do arrive, there are a number of rituals that must be gone through before the business part of a meeting can start: first, the small talk, a necessary part of all personal encounters; then, the customary tea or other drink, followed perhaps by talk about family and personal problems; and finally, the business of the day. All this takes time and usually does not start before ten o'clock in the morning.

The business part of the talk will also be lengthy because important issues are approached in a roundabout rather than direct manner. Impatient Americans will wonder when the key issues of the meeting will be discussed. And after the meeting has concluded and the visitor believes he has agreement to proceed, nothing may happen for weeks, or months, or ever.

For Russians, time is not measured in minutes or hours but more likely in days, weeks, and months. The venerated virtue in Russia is not punctuality but patience. As a student from India who had spent four years in Moscow advised me, "Be patient, hope for the best, but prepare for the worst. Everything here takes time and sometimes never gets done."

Americans are oriented toward doing; Russians, toward thinking. As a Russian psychiatrist explained to me, "Russians can look at an object all day and reflect on it but take no action." When faced with an issue to be resolved, they will first think through the historical, philosophical, and ideological considerations as well as the consequences of whatever is to be decided. Americans will first consider the practical points, the obstacles to be overcome, the details, and how to get from here to there.

A Russian conference interpreter, recalling her experience with Russians and Americans in the evenings after their formal meetings had ended, told me: "The Russians would sit all night drinking tea, discussing and reflecting, while the Americans would be thinking about what they had to do the next day and preparing to do it."

Such divergent views of time can create difficulties in cooperative efforts and joint ventures. Americans will want to negotiate an agreement quickly, schedule an early start on the venture, begin on time, complete the work as expeditiously as possible, and show early results or profit. Russians will need more time to get organized, and there will be frequent delays and postponements. They will be less concerned with immediate results, and profit is a concept that they are only beginning to understand. The job may be completed but only after considerable prodding from the American side.

What to do? Not much, except to persist patiently and speak softly, but carry a big prod.

The Russian Language

> The Russian language surpasses all European languages, since it has the magnificence of Spanish, the liveliness of French, the strength of German, the delicacy of Italian, as well as the richness and conciseness of Greek and Latin.
>
> —M. V. Lomonosov

The most successful Americans in understanding the Russians, as readers will have noted by now, are those who speak some Russian. Russian speakers, whether they be businesspeople, journalists, scholars and scientists, professional or citizen diplomats, all have a significant advantage. Communication may be possible through smiles, hand signals, body language, and interpreters, but the ability to carry on a conversation in Russian raises the relationship to a more meaningful level.

Americans who are put off by the challenge of studying Russian should know that it is far easier to learn than many other languages, such as Chinese, Arabic, or Finnish. Russians are not offended by foreigners with an inadequate command of Russian. Many of their non-Russian citizens also speak Russian poorly.

The study of Russian in the United States is increasing. In the 1989-1990 school year, there was a 40 percent increase in the number of students enrolled in precollege study of Russian.[23] The total number (17,856) was still small, and a recent study showed that there were more teachers of English in the Soviet Union than students of Russian in the United States. But the increase does reflect the rising interest in Russian study as interaction between the two countries increases.

Russian is a Slavic language, together with Ukrainian, Belarusian, Polish, Czech, Slovak, Bulgarian, and several other related tongues. These are all Indo-European languages, a group which includes, among others, the Germanic, Romance, and English languages, and all have common roots.

Russian and English with common roots? While this at first may seem difficult to imagine, Russian and English do have some cognates—related words with a common root. That most basic word *milk*, for example, is a cognate to the Russian *moloko*. Compare also *apple* with the Russian *yabloko*. And many English words, previously unknown in Russia, have recently come into common usage, such as *test*, *briefing*, and *parking*, although they are given a Russian pronunciation, and often a Slavic ending. More English words will be acquired as contact between Russians and Americans increases.

It takes about 10 percent longer to say something in Russian than in English, and experienced translators say that they will often need three or more Russian words for one English word. Add to this the Russian tendency to be long-winded—a characteristic of agricultural societies, the old American South included—and you have another reason for Russian verbosity.

Another difficulty with Russian results from the shifting accentuation of words. There is no general rule on where the stress falls in a sentence, as there is in most European languages. A Russian word placed at the beginning of a sentence will have more importance than when placed at the end.

The Cyrillic alphabet, derived from the Greek and named after St. Cyril who devised it for Slavic languages, may also faze some Americans. Russian, however, is pronounced as it is written. If you can read it, you can pronounce it. This gives Russian an advantage over English, in which words are seldom pronounced as they are written.

Americans who do not speak Russian should at least learn the alphabet before traveling to Russia. Knowing the thirty-two letters of the Cyrillic alphabet will enable travelers to read signs, menus, and the names of Metro stations, and will considerably facilitate their stay. It will also give them a start in building a Russian vocabulary.

Russian has numerous words acquired from Western languages. Many mechanical, medical, and technical terms are from German; artistic and cultural words from French; and business and modern scientific terms from English. Moreover, many of those long and imposing Russian words are structured exactly as their Western equivalents. A basic vocabulary can be easily acquired by learning a few root words and the Russian equivalents of English prefixes, suffixes, and prepositions.

Words are inflected, as in Latin and German, to denote such distinctions as case, gender, number, tense, person, and mood. And Russian verbs have two aspects: the imperfective for repeated actions and the perfective for completed actions. Hingley wonders, facetiously, whether it is not this strict separation of these two aspects of the verb that makes it so difficult for Russians to complete actions.[24]

The grammar sounds complex, and it is, but there are a few rules that explain it all. Although Russian can be learned cold, it helps to know another inflected European language.

Russian is replete with negatives, and positive ideas are often expressed negatively. An object will be "not big" rather than "small." A Russian will describe his or her feelings as "not bad" rather than "good." And a double negative in Russian does not make an affirmative as in English, but emphasizes the negative. The more negatives in a sentence, the more negative the meaning.

One final caveat: while Russian has its share of earthy and vulgar expressions, they are not used in polite society.

Misunderstandings

Russian is a very rich language. In English one word may suffice to convey an idea, while Russian will have several words to choose from, each with a slightly different shade of meaning.

This presents problems for interpreters and translators, as well as possibilities for misunderstandings.

Many words and expressions in one language simply do not exist in the other. Aleksei Mikhalev, a Russian translator of American literature, says that differences in language and literature—two significant products of a nation's thought and psychology—demonstrate that Americans and Russians are not very much alike. He cites the impossibility of finding precise Russian equivalents for the simple English word *privacy*, a concept which does not exist in Russian or in many other languages as well. Other untranslatables from English to Russian listed by Mikhalev include *take care, have fun, make love, efficiency,* and *challenge.*[25]

Even translatable words are sometimes mistranslated, especially when dialect or idiomatic language is involved. Kornei Chukovsky, one of the best translators from English into Russian, cites several such bloopers. In one, an experienced Russian translator, in translating a work by American poet Langston Hughes, wrote about the passionate love of a black man for a black woman who had rejected him. Actually, Hughes had written about a "Black Maria" (police van) that he hoped was not coming to get him. Another example cited by Chukovsky, from Galsworthy's *Forsythe Saga*, had a young man, Michael Mont, in a boat with his girlfriend, rowing across a river when he suddenly "caught a crab" (a rowing term indicating a faulty stroke). The Russian translator had Mont fishing for crabs in the middle of an ardent conversation with his sweetheart.[26]

A seemingly simple expression can have one meaning in English and another in Russian, as I learned when helping to arrange the first loan between a Soviet and an American museum. In 1973 Washington's National Gallery of Art sought to borrow a Rembrandt from a Moscow museum. In the spirit of detente, the Soviet government agreed to lend the work, but it first sought assurance that the U.S. government would guarantee the security of the valuable Rembrandt while it was in the United States.

In response to an official request for a guarantee, I informed the Soviet cultural attaché that the State Department would take "all possible measures" to safeguard the Rembrandt. This was boilerplate used to indicate that the department would do all it possibly could—in this case merely requesting the museum and local government authorities to take appropriate measures to protect the Rembrandt. The Soviet diplomat then asked, in Russian, whether this meant *vsyo vozmozhno* (everything possible), an expression that is stronger in Russian than in English, with the emphasis on "everything." I repeated, in English, that the State Department would take all possible measures. My Soviet colleague accepted this as vsyo vozmozhno, which satisfied Moscow's needs. Had the Rembrandt been damaged or stolen, it might have been the end of his career, and mine.

To prevent misunderstandings, Americans who are planning to make an oral presentation in Russia should prepare a paper in advance containing its main points. A written statement will help to avoid the hazards of interpreting as well as the tendency of Russians to think in general rather than specific terms. Presenting a paper will also ensure that they will know exactly what the Americans intended to say, regardless of what was actually said and how it was translated into Russian.

Talk comes naturally to Russians, and every Russian seems to be a born orator. Conversations begin easily between complete strangers as well as between men and women. The complexities of the language notwithstanding, it can be a pleasure to listen to Russian speech. Delivery is unhurried—often eloquent—and without pretense. But Russians can also talk around a difficult issue without addressing it directly. Listeners should pay close attention to what is left unsaid in addition to what is said.

Don't expect short responses to simple questions. Rather than respond with a brief yes or no, Russians are more likely to give a lengthy explanation that will leave the listener wondering whether the answer is indeed yes or no.

Body language is important. Russians use hands and facial expressions to convey ideas and emotions in contrast to Anglo-

Saxons, who consider such demeanor distracting if not unmannerly. Through body language, a person's intent can be determined without even understanding the words. One Russian diplomat I negotiated with would remain impassive throughout each session. But when we reached an issue that was difficult for him, his face would become florid and a vein on the side of his head would palpitate.

Physical contact by Russians—touching another person—is a sign that things are going well and a degree of rapport has been reached. The degree of physical contact will indicate how well things are going. Placing a hand on another person's arm, for example, or embracing someone are good signs.

Facial expressions are also clues to behavior. Americans are taught to open conversations with smiles and to keep smiling. Russians tend to start out with grim faces, but when they do smile, it reflects relaxation and progress in developing a good relationship. Winks and nods are also good signs. If a stony look continues, though, you are not getting through and are in trouble.

Proximity to other persons, as noted above, is much more common in Russia—and in many other cultures—than in the West. Russians stand very close when conversing, often less than twelve inches, which is closer than most Americans will find comfortable. They gesticulate more and do not hesitate to make physical contact and invade the other person's space.

An American teacher of Russian recalls how, during study at Moscow State University, a Russian instructor playfully rapped the knuckles of some Americans in his class as a sign of displeasure over their inadequate preparation for the day's lesson:

> The American men, in an uproar at both the teacher's invasion of their space and his use of body contact to enforce his wishes, went immediately after class to the director to complain about the instructor's behavior... As a result, the instructor was reprimanded and told to maintain "a proper distance" from his students and to refrain from all physical contact with Americans, "who do not understand these things."[27]

Straight talk is appreciated, even when it leads to disagreement. But when disagreement does occur, Russians appreciate honesty rather than attempts to paper over differences. It is far better to level with them and be certain that they fully understand your position. In debate they respect adversaries who are straightforward and sincere in expressing views that diverge from their own. "The Russian is never more agreeable than after his knuckles have been sharply rapped," writes George F. Kennan. "He takes well to rough play and rarely holds grudges over it."[28]

Confrontations over differences of views can often be avoided by letting Russians talk themselves out. After they have unburdened themselves and expressed their righteousness and indignation, their opposition may moderate and the differences may turn out to be not as great as originally believed. In fact, after talking themselves out, Russians and Americans may even find that they have a unanimity of views.

Nyet is a simple Russian word that is often misunderstood. Nyet seems to be an almost automatic response by officials or service personnel when asked if something can be done or whether a product is available in a store, a table in a restaurant, or a dish on a menu. Clerks, doormen, waiters, and others seem to prefer the easy response—nyet.

There can be several reasons for the automatic nyet. One common response is, "We don't do it that way here." The item requested in a store or restaurant may indeed not be available. Or the clerk may not care whether it is available, or may not be at all interested in helping the customer. In any event, Russians do not routinely accept a nyet, nor should a foreign visitor. Keep talking, smile, don't get upset, don't raise your voice, and keep repeating your request. As noted before, a good interpersonal relationship can often overcome the obstacle, whatever it may be, and beat the system.

A nyet, however, when expressed in a manner indicating that the real response is "perhaps," may indicate that a little incentive is needed. In such cases, a pack of American cigarettes or a few American dollars, discreetly brought into view, will produce the desired effect.

The Telephone

> Telephones in Russia are enough to make the most patient man curse.
> —Irving R. Levine, *Main Street, U.S.S.R.*

Irving R. Levine was NBC correspondent in Moscow in the 1950s, but his description of the Soviet telephone system is still valid; and the cursing continues.

To make a telephone call in Russia is not simple. The system is primitive, the technology archaic, and many nonofficial persons do not have telephones. On most local calls one must shout to be heard, and a friendly conversation can become a shouting match.[29]

In a culture that values personal relations, communicating is best done face-to-face. Russians relate well to people but not through letters, telegrams, or even telephones—another legacy of life in the village. Letters are answered late, if at all. Telegrams and telexes may get a better response, but this is by no means assured. Facsimile and electronic mail are recent innovations and not yet available everywhere. Doing business with Russians from a distance is difficult. So what happens when one attempts to use the telephone, the preferred medium for communication in the West?

In Russian offices there are no procedures for transferring a call to another phone. When a call is made—let's say to Ivanov (Johnson)—his receptionist or secretary cannot pick up the phone, take the message, and transfer the call to Ivanov if he is there. Ivanov's telephone connects to him and to him only. It sits on his desk and only he can answer it. If he is not in, the phone will ring forever and no one else will answer it since it is Ivanov to whom the caller obviously wishes to speak. (One number that does answer in Moscow is the American Embassy,

252-2451, which has someone on duty around the clock. In St. Petersburg, the number for the American Consulate General is 274-8235.)

It is prudent to know the telephone numbers of persons you need to contact and to keep these numbers in a safe place. For many years there was no Moscow telephone directory. More recently, telephone directories for business and state offices (but not residences) have been published in some large citites. Directories, however, are not always up-to-date because numbers change frequently. Directory assistance for Russian speakers is available in Moscow by dialing 09 but, again, not for residences. Hotels for foreigners will usually have a Service Bureau where telephone numbers may also be obtained. Before departing for Moscow, it is advisable to obtain from earlier travelers the numbers of people you will be trying to call. And when in Moscow, a little black book will be useful to record the numbers you will be collecting. Bear in mind also that public telephones operate only with a *dvushka* (a two-kopeck piece). Russians always carry a few of them, for they are hard to come by.

When you do get through to Ivanov, he may seem abrupt or noncommittal. Russians are not accustomed to doing business by phone because the service is bad and they know that the phone may be bugged. If you are able to agree on a time and place for a meeting, your call will have been a success.

If Ivanov is important, he will have more than one phone on his desk, and his importance may be judged by the number of phones. I have seen as many as five on one desk, and wondered what happened when several rang at the same time.

One Soviet writer's surprise reaction to how Americans use the telephone tells us as much about Russia as about America. After visiting the United States, he wrote:

One rarely hears of business meetings in the United States. All matters are settled straightaway on the spot, by telephone. Whichever establishment you call you may be sure that the man you want will be available. If, for some important reason, he's not there, a secretary will answer and will always tell you affably and politely who can help you instead, or will tell you exactly when the person you need will be back and when you should call him. The most complex questions are settled by telephone."[30]

Russians and Americans

> You Russians and we Americans! Our countries so distant, so unlike at first glance—such a difference in social and political conditions, and our respective methods of moral and practical development the last hundred years;—and yet in certain features, and vastest ones, so resembling each other.
>
> —Walt Whitman, *Letter to a Russian*

Despite Russia's ambivalence toward the West, Russians admire Americans as people. Notwithstanding the political and ideological differences and the often diametrically opposed values of the two societies, Russians bear no ill will toward Americans. In fact, they like us.

"The foreign country in which the majority of Russians, and perhaps the Soviet Government, are most interested is America," writes Sir William Hayter, British Ambassador to Moscow in the 1950s. "It is the goal they are constantly being urged, or urging themselves, to 'catch up and overtake.' They share many tastes with it—love of gadgets, technology, massive scale... America is their favorite foreign country."[31]

During my own two years in Moscow with the American Embassy at the height of the Vietnam War, I never once met a Russian who held anything against me as an American. How could this be, given our differences and the steady stream of anti-American propaganda that Russians were fed in their media over so many decades?

To begin, the effect of anti-American propaganda should be discounted. Until glasnost, few Russians believed what their media told them. If news was official, it was doubted; if a rumor, it was believed. Russians have had good reason to question official pronouncements.

In a country whose thousand-year history records one war after another—and with immense suffering—Russians know that they have never had a war with the United States. They also know that Russians and Americans were allies against their most recent enemy, Germany, in two world wars. Moreover, there are no territorial disputes between the two countries, a common cause of conflict.

Russia and America have no trade rivalries, nor do they compete in world markets. Many Russians remember the aid they received from the United States—in the famine of the 1920s, the industrialization of the 1920s and early 1930s, and the lend-lease of the 1940s during the darkest days of their life-and-death struggle with Nazi Germany. Indeed, some Soviet military vehicles were commonly known in Russian as Willys and Studebakers because the first jeeps and trucks to arrive from the United States during the war bore the names of those companies.

Fascination with machinery is shared by Russians and Americans. The best way to start a conversation with Russians, I learned in Moscow, was to open the hood of my American station wagon on a downtown street and start tinkering with the engine. Immediately, I would be surrounded by a crowd asking how many "horses" the engine had, how fast the car could go, how much gas it used (in liters per hundred kilometers), and how much it cost.

But to go beyond casual conversations and really get to know Russians, it is necessary to sit down with them and eat and drink together. The best conversations with Russians occur, as earlier noted, at the kitchen table. The highlight of a visit to the United States by a delegation of senior Soviet officials in the 1970s occurred when they sat around a kitchen table with American farmers in the Midwest and discussed farming far into the night.

I had a similar experience once when I dropped in unannounced at the library of the Siberian Academy of Sciences in Novosibirsk. Identifying myself as the Cultural Counselor of the American Embassy, I asked to see the library director. Surprised by the unexpected visit of an American diplomat, he graciously ushered me into his office. The legendary Russian hospitality soon showed itself when he sent an assistant out to get something for us to eat. She returned shortly with a long spicy sausage, a loaf of good black bread, a bottle of vodka, and an old kitchen knife; and our conversation warmed with our stomachs as we sat at his desk eating and drinking—without plates, forks, or napkins—and discussing libraries and book exchanges between our two countries.

America's power and size also attract Russians—the "big is beautiful" syndrome. Russians see themselves and Americans as citizens of two great powers destined to play leading roles on the world stage. As a Russian professor explained to me: "We have more in common with Americans than with West Europeans. Both our countries have no aristocracies, both are big and without the complexes of small nations."

Joint endeavors between Russians and Americans are therefore seen as natural. Indeed, Russians get a psychological lift from working with Americans, regarding such cooperation as recognition of their coequal status. But they also expect Americans to accept them as equals, to return their admiration, and they are disappointed and puzzled when we do not.

Russians are very curious about the United States, and there is no country they wish to visit more. Many exciting innovations in their drab lives have come from America—jazz, jeans, rock music, Pepsi, and now Big Macs, to name a few. Russians who are able to visit America are astounded by the abundance and high standard of living. On seeing their first American supermarket, many have believed it to be a "Potemkin village," a setup created to impress foreigners. Others, confused by the choices offered consumers, have questioned the need for so many different brands of the same products.

Fascination with Western products is common. If an item is from the West, especially the United States, it is assumed to be better and worth a premium price. Tourists in Russia will be accosted and asked if they want to sell articles of clothing they are wearing. One Russian diplomat in Washington boasted to me that he had an American bathroom in his Moscow apartment, purchased at Hechinger, a Washington-area building supplies and hardware chain. During several years abroad he had managed to purchase all the bathroom essentials and ship them back to Moscow.

Russians recognize that Americans are far richer than they are, but they resent being talked down to. While Russians themselves are outspokenly critical of their own society, they can be hypersensitive to criticism by a foreigner. As one Russian teacher told me, "We think of America as the rich cousin who has material wealth meeting Russia, the poor cousin, who has spiritual wealth. We are envious of your material wealth, but don't flaunt it. We know you have it."

But much of what Russians see in the United States confuses them. Puzzling are the free choices Americans have, the seeming lack of order, the concern for individual rights, the crime and decay of our great cities, and the decentralization of the economy. Indeed, some Russians, after touring the United States, have been certain that there must be some secret center which controls and runs the economy. How else could it perform so well?

To Americans, Russians are also puzzling. Why is it so difficult and time-consuming to reach agreement with them? Why do they always seem to be delaying decisions instead of being reasonable and meeting us halfway? Why are they so mistrustful of others, and can they be trusted to honor agreements?

For Americans, the segregation of foreigners and the special treatment given them may be puzzling. In domestic airports, for example, there are special waiting rooms for foreigners. The isolation of foreigners seems strange today, but there is a historical precedent. In medieval Moscow foreign residents were also segregated in certain quarters of the city. Today, there are special hotels for foreign tourists to which Russians are denied entrance as well as shops with hard-to-find items for persons with foreign currency.

Russians do not resent special privileges for foreigners because they regard them as signs of courtesy and hospitality. They very much resent, however, privileges and special treatment for their own officials.

Despite some similarities, Russians and Americans are indeed different, Walt Whitman's words notwithstanding. Understanding the differences is the first step to bridging them.

"Be patient with us," a Russian newspaper editor counseled me, "America has had glasnost for two hundred years; we are only now beginning to have it. Many things are difficult to change. We cannot yet make all those changes, but we are savoring the opportunity to try."

---

[1]Stites, *Revolutionary Dreams*, 244.

[2]Inge Morath and Arthur Miller, *In Russia* (New York: Viking, A Studio Book, 1969), 15.

[3]Hingley, *Russian Mind*, 179.

[4]Stites, *Revolutionary Dreams*, 244-45.

[5]Murray Feshbach, testimony at hearing on *A Changing Soviet Society*, before the Commission on Security and Cooperation in Europe, CSCE 101-1-4, 17 May 1989 (Washington, DC: U.S. Government Printing Office, 1989), 11.

[6]*New York Times*, 9 July 1989.

[7]Mikhail Heller and Aleksander M. Nekrich, *Utopia in Power, The History of the Soviet Union from 1917 to the Present* (New York: Simon and Schuster, Summit Books, 1986), 508.

[8]Aksyonov, *Melancholy Baby*, 77.

[9]*Parade Magazine*, 8 Oct. 1989, 27.

[10]Morath and Miller, *In Russia*, 15.

[11]Nina Belyaeva, quoted by Georgie Anne Geyer, "...wrong basket?," *Washington Times*, 31 May 1990.

[12]Stites. Interview with author, 11 February 1991.

[13]Hosking, *Awakening of the Soviet Union*, 13.

[14]Vaclav Havel, acceptance speech on receiving the Peace Prize of the German Booksellers Association on 15 October 1989, translated by A. G. Brain, *New York Review of Books* (18 Jan. 1990): 8.

[15]Custine, *Empire of Czar*, 437.

[16]Andrei Sinyavsky [Abram Tertz, pseud.], "Thought Unaware," *New Leader* 48, no. 15 (19 July 1965): 19.

[17]Hedrick Smith, *The Russians* (New York: New York Times Book Company, Quadrangle, 1976), 120-21.

[18]Feshbach, *Changing Soviet Society*, 12.

[19]Marshall I. Goldman, "Gorbachev at Risk," *World Monitor* (June 1990): 38.

[20]For this quote (as well as other material on *vranyo*) I am indebted to Hingley, *Russian Mind*, 91, and Hingley, "That's No Lie, Comrade," *Problems of Communism* 11, no. 2 (1962): 47-55.

[21]Fyodor Dostoyevsky, "A Word or Two About Vranyo," *Diary of A Writer*, quoted by Hingley, *Russian Mind*, 105.

[22]Hingley, "That's No Lie," 54.

[23]From a report by The Russian Studies Center for Secondary Schools, Choate Rosemary Hall, Wallingford, Connecticut, 1990.

[24]Hingley, *Russian Mind*, 206.

[25]Lourie and Mikhalev, "Why You'll Never Have Fun in Russian," 38.

[26]Kornei Chukovsky, *The Art of Translation*, translated by Lauren G. Leighton (Knoxville: University of Tennessee Press, 1984), 11-12.

[27]Barbara Monahan, *A Dictionary of Russian Gesture* (Tenafly, NJ: Hermitage, 1983), 15.

[28]George F. Kennan, *Memoirs, 1925-1950* (Boston: Little, Brown and Company, 1967), 564.

[29]Some of the material on telephones has been drawn from "Nina Bouis' Report from Moscow," *The Soros Foundation Newsletter* 1, no. 6 (1989).

[30]Albertas Laurinciukas, "How I Failed to Find the Average American," *Soviet Writers Look at America*, edited by Alexander Fursenko (Moscow: Progress Publishers, 1977), 175.

[31]Sir William Hayter, *The Kremlin and the Embassy* (London: Hodder and Stoughton, 1966), 133.

6

Negotiating with Russians

If there are found among the Russians, better diplomatists than among other nations...it is because our journals inform them of every thing which is done or projected among ourselves, and because instead of prudently disguising our weaknesses, we display them, with passion, every morning; whilst, on the contrary, the Byzantine policy of the Russians, working in the dark, carefully conceals from us everything that is thought, done, or feared among them. We march exposed on all sides, they advance under cover. The ignorance in which they leave us blinds our view; our sincerity enlightens theirs; we suffer from all the evils of idle talking, they have all the advantages of secrecy; and herein lies all their skill and ability....
—Custine, *Empire of the Czar*

The Art of Negotiation

Don't hurry to reply, but hurry to listen.
—Russian proverb

Negotiation is an art well known to diplomats, lawyers, and business executives. Two parties meet, each with its own objectives, and attempt to reach a mutually acceptable agreement which will satisfy their needs. The goal for each side is to gain as much as possible while giving up only what is necessary to reach agreement. At this age-old game the Russians are experts.

Where the two sides have similar goals, as is often the case when negotiations are entered into willingly, the process can be relatively easy. Both sides seek to reach agreement and have hopes of doing so; otherwise, they would not have agreed to meet. But when Russians and Americans negotiate, there are often considerations that may make it difficult to agree.

For the United States and Russia, the negotiation of minor issues may be amplified out of proportion, thereby making minor issues appear more important than they really are. Agreement in principle—on broad objectives—may be easy to reach, but how the agreement will be carried out—the details of implementation—are usually more difficult. Long-standing policy may have to be modified by one side or the other. The terms of the agreement must satisfy the legal, political, and ideological requirements of both sides—yes, Americans may also have ideological requirements. And the subject under negotiation may be related to other issues for which one side or the other may not wish to establish a precedent. Most Americans who negotiate with Russians represent only themselves or their organizations, while the Russians in most negotiations represent their government.

Russian negotiators are likely to be under strict instructions and without the flexibility of their American opposites to make on-the-spot decisions. Where the negotiators represent cooperatives or other private entities, they will have more flexibility.

The greatest challenge, however, results from the different Russian and American approaches to negotiations. Americans generally regard compromise as desirable and inevitable, a logical way of doing business—meet them halfway and make a deal. Americans, consequently, regard any inability to reach agreement easily and quickly as failure. Russians regard compromise as a sign of weakness, a retreat from a correct and morally justified position. Russians, therefore, are great "sitters," prepared to wait out their opposite numbers in the expectation that time and Russian patience will produce more concessions from the impatient Americans. Soviet Foreign Minister Molotov was dubbed "Stonebottom" because of his ability to outsit the other side.

Chess is a Russian national pastime, and Russians negotiate in the same way they play chess, planning several moves ahead. Americans should think through the consequences of each move before making it since it may establish a precedent that the Russians will cite later on, or it may lead to a tack in the negotiations different from the one expected.

Russian negotiating teams are usually composed of veterans who negotiate year-round with representatives of other countries. Americans, products of a mobile society, are more likely to be new to their positions and less experienced in the art of negotiation, particularly with Russians.

A concept or word from one side of the table may not be understood by the other because it simply does not exist in the other side's politics, laws, culture, or even language. Add to this the limitations to what Americans and Russians know and understand about each other, and the task of negotiating with the Russians becomes even more challenging.

Equality, reciprocity, and mutual advantage are watchwords that need to be kept in mind. Russians and Americans negotiate as equals, as befits great powers, and Russians are very sensitive to any intimations that they are not being treated with sufficient respect and dignity. Agreements reached should provide for reciprocity—what is done in one country should be matched by similar action in the other, and under conditions as equal as possible. And most important, the benefits to each side should be comparable.

The negotiations can be lengthy, tedious, and demanding. Negotiation, however, is the only way to do business with Russians, and Americans should understand the basic rules of the game before entering the playing field.

Procedures and Tactics

Where there is sense, there is order.

—Russian proverb

The first step in any negotiation is to know what you want. This may sound overly simple but often it is not. Many negotiators go into meetings without knowing precisely what their objectives are. Americans had better think through their objectives and define them clearly, because the Russians will certainly know their own.

Next, draft the text of an agreement that includes all your objectives. This is your maximum position—what you ideally would like to see in the final document. The Russians will also have their draft, with their objectives, and it will represent their maximum position. Each side should understand that this is merely the opening bid—as in an Eastern bazaar—and neither should expect the other to accept the initial draft which it has placed on the table. To save time, drafts may be exchanged in advance of the actual negotiations so that each side may study the other's objectives and draft language and be better prepared to negotiate.

Russian negotiating strategy reflects differences in thought patterns between East and West. Western negotiators prefer a pragmatic and detailed approach, taking up one issue at a time and progressing systematically toward a final agreement. Russians prefer a more general and conceptual approach.

In political negotiations, for example, Russians will often seek agreement "in principle" which will be in harmony with an ideological framework or universal outlook. Such an agreement, which provides greater flexibility when the time for implementation arrives, will include high-sounding ideals couched in lofty language but little specificity. Americans should start with simple proposals and develop the complexities later, but not so late that they may be considered by the Russians to be of insufficient importance to be taken seriously.

In commercial negotiations or where money is involved, Russians will be sticklers for details, insisting on a more detailed contract than is usual in international business. This is particularly true when a negotiation involves *valyuta* (hard currency, i.e., dollars). Because hard currency is in short supply, Russian negotiators will be very reluctant to expend dollars but most eager to accept them. In joint commercial ventures, they will make it difficult, if not impossible, for foreign investors to repatriate their profits in hard currency.

The protocol of who sits where at the negotiating table should be observed. The Russian head of delegation may sit at the center of the table, flanked on both sides by an interpreter and aides in descending order of rank. Or the chairperson may sit at the head of the table. Whatever the arrangement, Americans should match it, with their chairperson seated across from their Russian opposite number. Russians are very status conscious. The two chairpersons should be of comparable rank, and a high-ranking visitor will be taken more seriously.

In their opening statements, Russians will provide a philosophical or ideological basis for their negotiating position. The opening statement may also provide clues to specific positions they will later take and reveal previously unstated objectives or difficulties that were not anticipated.

In the "give and take" of negotiations, Russians will attempt to size up their opposite numbers. Who is this man? Is he serious? Can we trust him? Is he strong? In making this assessment, Russians, like boxers, will bob and weave, feint, probe for weaknesses, and press forward vigorously when they sense a willingness to accommodate their views. When a probe meets with resistance, they will pull back.

Russian delivery style can be dramatic and emotional, intended to demonstrate true commitment to the position being espoused, and they may use tough talk to beat down adversaries. Russians can raise their voices, express indignation, and imply threats. This should be seen for what it actually is—theatrics—although it also reflects a propensity for power plays.

Americans can respond in two ways. They may allow the Russians to speak their piece, hear them out, enjoy the performance, and respond in a firm but calm manner. Alternatively, Americans may elect to talk tough themselves, which Russians will understand and respect as an indication of resolve and determination. Because he did not understand this, President Kennedy gave Premier Khrushchev the impression, when they met in Vienna in 1961, that he was weak and could be intimidated by the emplacement of Soviet missiles in Cuba.

In most negotiations Russians maintain strict discipline and speak with one voice, that of their delegation chairperson. An exception to this rule may be found in commercial or other negotiations where several government ministries or agencies are represented on the Russian side, along with "end-users." Americans, by contrast, tend to speak with many voices, reflecting the pluralism of U.S. society as well as disparate views within the delegation. This confuses Russians because they do not know which American is speaking with authority.

The most difficult part of a negotiation, Americans often report, is reaching agreement among the various viewpoints and interests of their own side. Any such differences should be resolved in advance, and Americans should speak with one voice at the negotiating table, remembering their national motto, *E pluribus unum*.

Russians will usually request that official negotiations, or at least plenary sessions (with full delegations), be conducted in two languages, Russian and English, even when the Russian negotiators speak English well. The Russian government regards Russian as a world language, on a par with English. The French and many others do the same. In small working groups, however, negotiations may be held in English.

One or more members of the U.S. delegation should be designated note takers. Not everything that is said will have to be recorded, but it will prove useful to have a written record, particularly on issues that are unresolved. A note taker who knows Russian will have two advantages. First, all Russian statements will be heard twice, once in the original Russian and again in English translation, thus giving the note taker more time to write and to be certain that what is recorded is correct. Second, nuances in Russian may not come through in the English translation.

Interpreters vary in quality and consistency in both countries and can be a source of misunderstanding. It is helpful to have someone on the U.S. delegation who is conversant in Russian and can monitor the interpreting.

Patience is a Russian virtue that pays off in negotiations. When negotiating on home turf, Russians can afford to wait out the other side. For Americans, however, time is money and Moscow is not the most pleasant city in which to while away costly hours. Americans in Moscow may therefore be tempted to make concessions in order to reach agreement quickly and return home. Such temptations should be resisted. Conversely, Russians negotiating in the United States may wish to expedite an agreement, particularly if they are spending their own dollars for hotel and other costs.

Who goes first? Russians traditionally prefer to know the other side's position before giving their own. They can do this by accepting the Americans' draft in advance but pleading that their own is not yet ready to present in exchange. When Russians host a negotiation, they will usually invite the other side to speak first. There is no particular disadvantage in doing so if the general outline of what each side hopes to achieve is known, or if there is a unanimity of views in advance.

Surprises should be avoided, however. If there is some radically new idea to be proposed, it would be best to discuss it with the Russians informally, well in advance of the negotiations, thereby giving them time to study it and prepare a response. When presented with a new and unexpected proposal, Russians will have to retreat to a previous position while seeking instructions from higher up. And as former U.S. Ambassador to Moscow Llewellyn Thompson advised, "Don't maneuver the Russian bear into a corner from which there is no escape; in such a position he can become vicious."[1]

At the negotiating table the two drafts are compared, line by line, word for word. Wherever the language of the Russian and English drafts is identical or similar in meaning, agreement is reached and these paragraphs are set aside. Where the two drafts differ in substance, brackets are placed around the language in question and these differences remain to be negotiated. A Russian offer to negotiate and reach agreement on each article of the drafts seriatim (individually and in succession) should be politely declined. Instead, the two drafts should first be reviewed in their entirety to identify all differences before the actual negotiating begins. This will permit some bracketed passages to be traded off against others.

Where Russians make a concession—accepting the language of the U.S. draft—they will usually expect a corresponding concession in return, a quid pro quo in another part of the draft. Where such trade-offs occur, they should be of equal importance. Russians have been known to concede a minor point but then demand a major concession in exchange. To avoid this, agreement should be sought first on all minor differences between the two drafts. Major differences should be left to the final stage of the negotiation, the endgame.

Regarding concessions, negotiators should understand which side wants or needs the agreement more. That side, commonly referred to in French as the *demandeur*, would normally be expected to make more concessions.

Experienced negotiators will also include several "throwaways" in their draft. These are demands which they know in advance the other side cannot accept. At some stage of the negotiation these may be withdrawn in exchange for concessions by the other side.

The Endgame

The final stage of a negotiation, the endgame, is the most dramatic, similar to the final minutes of a close football game. The minor issues have been resolved but one or more major differences are still outstanding. The score is tied and one side digs in for a goal-line stand.

In such a situation Americans may be tempted to make concessions in order to end a lengthy negotiation and reach an agreement, which may be better than no agreement at all. If the issues in dispute are important, that temptation should be resisted. It should be made clear to the Russians that further concessions cannot be made and that it would be better to have no agreement than a poor one. In the endgame Russians will be firm but they can also change positions radically if they want an agreement and are persuaded that the other side will not retreat.

When an impasse is reached, it is advisable to present your bottom line, your basic requirements which must be satisfied in order to agree. The Russians will appreciate this, but they will, of course, have their own bottom line. The final agreement must reflect the bottom lines of both sides.

In the endgame, agreement on differences can often be reached away from the negotiating table at a working lunch or "a walk in the woods." The resolved issues should then be formally confirmed at the negotiating table.

At times a negotiator is able to agree to a particular point but may not be certain that the home office—government, board of directors, or financial backers—will also agree. In such cases, agreement can be reached "ad referendum," meaning that it is contingent upon agreement by higher authorities. For visitors to Moscow this can usually be accomplished with a telephone call or fax to the home office. Telephone calls, though, may be monitored.

The Paperwork

Don't brag about the deal until you get the seal.
— Russian proverb

Russians like to put agreements on paper, even on minor matters, duly signed by both parties, stating what has been agreed to and how it will be carried out. Even when formal agreement has not been reached, Russians will want to sign a *protokol*, a joint statement recording what has been discussed.

This is the Russian way, and it is almost impossible to avoid. Americans may wonder why they should sign something if no agreement has been reached. The protokol, however, can serve a useful purpose by providing a written record of what was discussed and agreed to, and not agreed to.

When agreement has finally been reached on all major issues, there is still much to be done. First, there is the usual cleanup work—small differences of substance in the English and Russian versions of the agreement which must be smoothed out. Second, the English and Russian versions of the agreed language must be reconciled.

Agreements customarily are signed in two versions, English and Russian, both equally valid. But to do this, someone on the American side who is fluent in Russian must sit down with a Russian who is fluent in English and compare the two language versions to make certain that what they say and mean is identical. This is not easily done because, as we have seen, there are many expressions in one language for which there are no exact equivalents in the other.

Major language differences can often be reconciled by minor changes in one language or the other. To be avoided, however, is the papering over of differences by saying that Americans will understand what is meant in English, and Russians will understand what is meant in Russian. Where such differences are substantial, they will inevitably resurface during implementation of the agreement and can be a source of future discord between the two parties. Where agreed language is ambiguous, Russians can be expected to interpret it in their favor.

As any lawyer will advise, read before you sign, and make certain that all language in the agreement is understood. Everything should be crystal clear, including who pays for what, a subject of importance to both sides.

And as lawyers will also advise, if the subject of the agreement is important or involves financial or legal obligations, have a lawyer review it before signing, even if that means reaching agreement ad referendum, i.e., initialing the document rather than signing, and signing later after the review has been completed.

Verification

> Trust, but verify.
> —Ronald Reagan (after an old Russian proverb)

Can Russians be trusted to honor commitments? The prudent response to this question—and to many other questions about Russia—is a "yes, but."

According to Zbigniew Brzezinski, Anglo-Saxons and Russians have different concepts of trust:

> The Anglo-Saxons approach these issues like negotiated, legal agreements. It might be called a litigational approach. To the Russians, a commitment is binding as long as it is historically valid, so to speak. And its historical validity depends on the degree to which that commitment is either self-enforcing or still mutually advantageous. If it ceases to be self-enforcing or mutually advantageous, it obviously has lapsed.[2]

To ensure that an agreement is observed, it is prudent to include a provision for regular review of implementation. This usually takes the form of periodic meetings of the two sides, held alternately in each country, to review past performance and make plans for the future. If such meetings are held, the agreement is more likely to be observed and not allowed to atrophy. As Ronald Reagan, recalling an old Russian proverb, repeatedly reminded Mikhail Gorbachev during their summit meetings, "Trust, but verify."

Related to verification are accountability and reporting, particularly where the expenditure of funds is involved. Russians are notoriously lax about accounting for expended funds and about using them effectively.

One of perestroika's best known slogans was *khozraschot*, usually translated as "cost accounting." The intent, however, was cost effectiveness, particularly in determining the real costs of producing goods and services. After sixty years of a command economy in which production costs were subsidized by the state, Russians have little experience in determining profit or loss. Under khozraschot, the objective was to make Russian enterprises self-sufficient by basing the prices of produced goods on true costs.

A related problem is accountability of funds. American donors of funds to Russian cultural and philanthropic institutions report difficulties in obtaining prompt and detailed reporting on how their funds are being expended. Some new foundations have scoffed at the standard regulatory and accounting procedures required by American donors. As one Russian foundation official put it, "We are all fine Christian men, and our [Russian] donors don't question what we do with their money."[3]

This response should not be seen as an intent to deceive but rather as a clash of cultures. Americans understand the need for accountability, annual financial reports, and audits by certified public accountants. But requesting such procedures from Russians may be seen as questioning their good faith and honesty. When encountering indignation over reporting requirements, Americans may wish to emulate Ronald Reagan by citing the old Russian proverb, "Trust, but verify."

Expect the Unexpected

One of the most significant features of Russian behavior ...[is] that abandonment to the thing in hand which makes it difficult for so many Russians to keep regular habits unless they are obliged, which makes them careless of detailed preparation...yet capable of bouts of long-continued activity which are beyond the endurance of the ordinary Westerner.

—Wright Miller, *Russians As People*

"In the United States," writes Rachel Connell, the Wellesley College student who spent a year in the Soviet Union, "when you follow the directions carefully...nine times out of ten things will work out as planned.... In the Soviet Union, people are suspicious of something they receive without a hassle."[4]

Things seldom go as planned with Russians. The will is there in most cases, but the bureaucracy is notoriously inefficient and its wheels turn slowly. A government which claims to give high priority to planning often inexplicably does things at the last minute, and without a plan. And the best-laid plans may not be carried out as intended, even when details are spelled out in agreements that have been negotiated and signed in good faith.

Russians often say, "In principle, it can be done." In practice, it often cannot. Russians begin discussions with generalities and leave the details to be dealt with later. And in their enthusiasm to reach agreement, officials tend to exaggerate the possibilities by signing agreements and making promises that offer more than they are actually able to deliver.

Of the 10,000 letters of intent that had been signed between Western companies and Soviet organizations since the start of perestroika, only some 1,500, by early 1990, had produced joint ventures registered with the Soviet authorities, and only about a hundred of these had actually begun operations.[5]

As Swedish lawyer Kaj Hober explains:

Western businessmen and their Soviet counterparts were anxious to negotiate deals and sign contracts and have them registered with the Ministry of Finance.... But then the parties had to begin worrying about the real work. What was each party in the deal supposed to do? Where would they get the raw materials? Which people in the project were going to do what? That's where we are now.[6]

Where should an American start in picking up the pieces after an agreement has fallen apart? Throughout this study, much has been made of the importance of the personal factor in doing business with Russians. For an agreement to be truly successful, there should be a personal relationship between an American on one side and a Russian on the other who both want to make something happen. When nothing happens—an agreement is not implemented—the American will have to return to the personal relationship. Reestablishing that relationship—by phone or another visit—can help to make something happen.

And some things happen without plan, as George Bush learned in May 1990 when Mr. Gorbachev, less than two weeks before his Washington summit meeting with Mr. Bush, unexpectedly made public his plans to also visit Minneapolis and California. The announcement created turmoil in the White House because the Kremlin had not presented an itinerary for the proposed coast-to-coast tour, hotel rooms had not been reserved in Minneapolis or California, and no provisions had been made for Mr. Gorbachev's security or for supplying the special fuel needed for his Aeroflot jet. As Andrew Rosenthal noted in the *New York Times*, "...even the most rudimentary preparations have not been made for the kind of cross-country trek that the White House would spend months planning."[7]

Failure to pin down details can also have unexpected consequences in cultural exchange. The first U.S.-Soviet cultural agreement, signed in 1958, provided for "sister university" relationships between universities in the two countries. Under the agreement, Indiana University was paired with Tashkent University.

The following year, a delegation from Tashkent arrived in Bloomington, Indiana, without advance notice, on the Friday afternoon of a football weekend when all hotel and motel rooms had been reserved. To make matters worse, the Soviets were without funds because they had flown from New York to Chicago, and then had spent all their dollars for a taxi to Bloomington, *Illinois*—right city, wrong state. Moreover, the letter from Moscow announcing their arrival plans was received at Indiana after the delegation had completed its visit and returned home.[8]

Thirty years later, in July 1989, hilarious history repeated itself. Five Soviet chefs in an exchange between U.S. and Soviet food professionals were lost for five hours in the New York City area. The Soviets had landed at Newark Airport while their American hosts were awaiting them at Kennedy Airport, where they were expected to arrive. Furthermore, the Soviets were originally scheduled to arrive, not in July but the previous October. Nevertheless, the Soviet and American chefs eventually found each other and were soon in the kitchen cooking things up together despite the misplaced and late arrival.[9]

Agreed timetables for action are often not complied with. Officials do not answer their mail promptly. The best way to get a decision or go-ahead is through a face-to-face meeting, which, of course, can mean a trip to Russia and added expense.

A trip to Novosibirsk in 1990 for a face-to-face meeting produced a surprise for one American from Minneapolis. After months of arranging his visit and confirming it by telex, the Twin Cities man traveled halfway around the world to meet a Russian fellow expert in the Siberian city, only to discover on arrival that his Russian colleague was in Minneapolis.[10]

Russian behavior can often be unpredictable. New initiatives are announced without adequate preparation, long-standing policies are suddenly and inexplicably reversed, and things do go wrong. As explained by Susan Hartman, codirector of Connect, U.S.-U.S.S.R., the Minneapolis group that arranged the Novosibirsk visit, "National organizations [in Russia] will disappear and reappear under different names with different people running them."[11] Americans, who are usually sticklers for planning, should be prepared to expect the unexpected.

What Americans can expect in business meetings is traditional Russian hospitality. The conference table will be laden with bottled water and soft drinks, cookies, and other sweets. Tea or coffee will be served. When an agreement or contract is signed, the signatories can expect to raise a glass of champagne. A festive lunch or dinner for visitors will usually be held at a well-known hotel or restaurant, with the customary four courses—zakuski, soup, main course, and dessert—and vodka and wine.

When Russians visit the United States, they expect the same treatment and are disappointed when their hospitality is not returned in the same degree. At the State Department, where funds for entertaining were negligible, we were always embarrassed when all we could offer our Russian visitors was coffee or tea in a styrofoam cup. (Americans who serve coffee or tea to Russians should be aware that drinks should always be served with something to eat, even if only a cookie.)

---

[1]Llewellyn Thompson, in his final briefing for American correspondents prior to departure from Moscow in 1968, a meeting which the author attended.

[2]Zbigniew Brzezinski. Interview with Radio Liberty-Radio Free Europe, quoted in *Wall Street Journal*, 25 March 1983.

[3]Sharon Tennison, Center for U.S.-U.S.S.R. Initiatives, San Francisco, California, in memo to U.S. foundations, 15 May 1990.

[4]Rachel Connell, *Crossways 1*, Newsletter of the American Collegiate Consortium for East-West Cultural and Academic Exchange Middlebury, Vermont (Spring 1991): 2.

[5]Keith A. Rosten, "Soviet Joint Ventures Riding on Troubled Waters," *Wall Street Journal*, 7 May 1990.

[6]Kaj Hober, quoted by Joel Kurtzman, "A Slowdown in Soviet Joint Ventures," *New York Times*, 15 April 1990.

[7]Andrew W. Rosenthal, "Gorbachev's Schedule, Anyone's Guess," *New York Times*, 20 May 1990.

[8]Robert F. Byrnes, *Soviet-American Academic Exchanges, 1958-1975* (Bloomington: Indiana University Press, 1976), 62-63.

[9]Marian Burros, "5 Russians Skirmish with a U.S. Kitchen and Everyone Wins," *New York Times*, 19 July 1989.

[10]"Soviet Exchanges with U.S. Booming," *New York Times*, 28 May 1990.

[11]Ibid.

7

Seeing the Real Russia

*They occupy your every moment; they distract your thoughts;
they engross your attention; they tyrannize over you by means
of officious politeness; they inquire how you pass your days;
they question you with an importunity known only to themselves, and by fete after fete they prevent you seeing their
country.*

—Custine, *Empire of the Czar*

Custine's frustrations over Russian hospitality have been shared
by many visitors since 1839. The Russian practice of keeping
visitors occupied round the clock is an old one, and obsession
with secrecy is often assumed to be the reason.

To be sure, a reformed KGB can still be expected to maintain
its vigilance in protecting state secrets from the eyes of curious
visitors from abroad. But while glasnost has made society more
open, Russian hosts persist in filling every available hour of a
visitor's time with sightseeing and other activities.

The explanation lies in the seriousness with which Russians
regard their obligations toward guests. One obligation is to be
certain that guests are kept busy and are not bored. Unfortunately, filling a visitor's schedule with sightseeing makes it more
difficult to see the real Russia, to the extent that is possible in
any large city today.

A visit to Russia should include more than a Kremlin tour, the Bolshoi Theater, the circus, museums, and other obligatory tourist sights. Visitors should try to learn how Russians live, and this can be done without having Russian friends or knowing the language. Bed-and-breakfast services are now available, and visitors can also break off from guided tours and strike out on their own.

A department store is a good place to start. GUM, the Moscow tsarist-era store on Red Square, is conveniently located. Nearby is Dyetsky Mir (Children's World), across from the Lubyanka, the KGB headquarters that once housed an infamous prison. Note the prices of the merchandise as well as the quality, but don't attempt to convert the prices to dollars. Exchange rates fluctuate. More important is what the ruble cost of an item will be to Russians who do not have dollars, and whether the item continues to be available to shoppers.

Try instead to figure what an item would cost Russian workers in terms of their monthly earnings. Wages rose rapidly in 1992 due to soaring inflation, but Russian hosts and guides will know what the average worker currently earns. Bear in mind that in mid-1992, according to official Russian statistics, nearly half of Russia's population was believed to be living below the poverty line.[1]

Visit a *gastronom* (state food store) to see what is being sold—what is not. Then go to one of the farmers' markets or privately-owned shops to see what is being sold on the free market, and compare the quality and prices. Check out the cost of bread–the staple of the Russian diet.

Railroad stations are a scene out of Old Russia. Each day some two million citizens swarm into Moscow on foraging trips from distances of up to a hundred miles to buy food that is not available in their hometowns. For the foreign tourist who will visit only Moscow or other large cities, these stations provide an opportunity to see common people from small towns and villages as well as the *bomzhi* (homeless) who are kept off the streets by the militia.

All of Moscow's several stations are accessible via the Metro (subway). The Petersburg, Kazan, and Yaroslav Stations are conveniently located adjacent to each other at the Komsomolskaya Metro stop. These stations have not changed much since Anna Karenina arrived by train from St. Petersburg.

The Metro is also a good place to see people. It is a model of efficiency and the best buy in town. A route map will make it easier to use.

Churches offer another glimpse of Old Russia as well as an opportunity to see the growing interest today in things Russian and spiritual. Of the 77,676 Russian Orthodox churches that existed before the Revolution, only some 7,500 remained in 1979.[2] Churches that have not been converted into museums are not easy to find, but many have reopened and Russians will be able to help locate them.

Moscow, of course, is not Russia, nor is St. Petersburg. Despite their many urban problems, these cities are the showcases of Russia, presenting the best that the nation has to offer in city living. The real Russia is to be found in the smaller cities, towns, and villages in which the bulk of the population lives, most of them off the beaten track in areas formerly closed to travel by foreign visitors and where the standard of living is much lower than in major cities.

The contrast between urban and rural life in Russia and America has been noted by Russian writer Vassily Aksyonov:

America's prosperity becomes apparent the moment you leave her large cities. In Russia the opposite is the case. What remains after the military has drained off most of the resources goes toward maintaining a minimal level of decency in the cities; the countryside and the villages are left to rot.[3]

---

[1]*Washington Post*, 21 July 1992.

[2]*A Chronicle of Russian Events*, nos. 40-42, Amnesty International Publications, London (1979): 125:.

[3]Aksyonov, *Melancholy Baby*, 30.

Epilogue

Whenever the right of speech shall be restored to this muzzled people, the astonished world will hear so many disputes arise, that it will believe the confusion of Babel again returned.

—Custine, *Empire of the Czar*

With free speech restored, the Russia of the 1990s is indeed a Babel of disputes, but also of creativity and new ideas. State control of information has been lifted and a younger generation has come of age, better educated than its elders, knowing more about Russia and the rest of the world, and with greater expectations for the future.

This generation gap has been described by Zbigniew Brzezinski, drawing on results of recent Russian public opinion polls:

> The older generation is confused, uneasy, frightened, less inclined to support change, and somewhat more ideologically oriented. The young people are now very much open minded on such things as communism versus capitalism and the free market initiative.... You also see it in the army. The young officers in a number of instances have sided with the democratic movements. The older officers are very worried.[1]

Reformers are attempting to establish a modern state and a civil society based on the rule of law. New political parties have emerged, and independent organizations are sanctioned by state authorities. Communist party control is a thing of the past.

Various solutions to the nationality problem are being debated. Some Russians still hope for a reconstitution of the imperium, dominated and led by Russians. Others foresee a loose confederation between Russia and the other republics, with increased autonomy for all. Still others are prepared to accept a new and sovereign Russian state, with the other republics free to go their own way.

Barriers to contacts with the outside world are crumbling, and Russia again has an opening to the West. International trade, joint economic ventures, cultural and scientific exchanges, and foreign travel are bringing Western ideas to a once-closed society.

Russia's first contacts with the West, in the early eighteenth century, began a long and slow process of Europeanization that eventually led to a flowering of creativity in the nineteenth century—Russia's golden age—in literature, music, and art. Contacts with the West also led to cautious attempts at reform of state and society. A second burst of creativity and reform occurred during the 1920s, following the revolution and civil war that had destroyed the old order and released the latent talent and creativity of Russians and other nationalities.

But the golden age was followed by World War I and revolution, and the creativity and reforms of the 1920s were stifled by a new ideology, Marxism-Leninism, and Stalin's terror. It is not unfair, therefore, to question what Russians will do this time with their newfound freedoms and renewed contacts with the West.

"Whatever happens," says George F. Kennan, "and whatever may be the fate of Gorbachev's efforts at the restructuring of Soviet society, Russia is, and is going to remain, a country very different from our own. We should not look for this difference to be overcome in any short space of time."[2]

Another guarded prognosis has been made by James Billington, Librarian of Congress and historian of Russian culture:

> No one can be sure of the outcome; and it is prudent to fear for the worst in the short run. But just as Soviet totalitarianism was something profoundly different from past absolutisms, so the post-totalitarian society that is emerging...is likely to be something totally new—perhaps a synthesis of a new Russian state within a loose, broader commonwealth and/or of liberal Western economic and political institutions with conservative Russian religious and cultural values."[3]

Whatever new Russia emerges from this time of turmoil, history tells us that it will be a product of many of the same forces that have shaped Russia in the past—geography, history, religion, culture, and governance. The new state will be neither European nor Asian, but uniquely Russian.

---

[1]Zbigniew Brzezinski, testimony at hearing on *Soviet Disunion: Creating a Nationalities Policy*, Subcommittee on European Affairs, Committee on Foreign Relations, U.S. Senate, 101st Cong., 2d sess., 1990. S. Hrg. 101-887, 13.

[2]George F. Kennan, "After the Cold War," *New York Times Magazine*, 5 Feb. 1989, 58.

[3]James H. Billington, testimony at hearing on *Soviet Disunion: Creating a Nationalities Policy*, Subcommittee on European Affairs, Committee on Foreign Relations, U.S. Senate, 101st Cong., 2d sess., 1990. S. Hrg. 101-887, 32.

Recommended Readings

Aksyonov, Vassily. *In Search of Melancholy Baby*. Translated by Michael Henry Heim and Antonina W. Bouis. New York: Vintage Books, 1989.

A celebrated Russian writer now living in the United States discovers his adopted land and contrasts it with the land of his birth.

Billington, James H. *The Icon and the Axe, An Interpretive History of Russian Culture*. New York: Random House, Vintage Books, 1970.

A detailed study of Russian culture from Kievan times to the post-Khrushchev era, by a leading American scholar of Russia.

Black, Cyril E. *Understanding Soviet Politics: The Perspective of Russian History*. Boulder: Westview Press, 1986.

A collection of essays on issues which shape our understanding of Soviet politics, by the late Princeton University historian, one of America's leading scholars of Russia.

Custine, Marquis de. *Empire of the Czar, A Journey Through Eternal Russia*. New York: Doubleday, Anchor Books, 1989.

The Russia of 1839, as seen by a French traveler. Later travelers to Russia have marveled at how little has changed since Custine.

Daniels, Robert V. *Russia, The Roots of Confrontation*. Cambridge: Harvard University Press, 1985.
A readable and reasoned account of Russian history, contemporary society, U.S.-Soviet relations, and of the manner in which Russia's past shapes the present and sets the terms for the future.

Ford, Robert A. D. *Our Man in Moscow, A Diplomat's Reflections on the Soviet Union*. Toronto: University of Toronto Press, 1989.
Diplomat, poet, and translator, Ford spent twenty-one years in the Soviet Union, including sixteen as Canadian ambassador.

Gray, Francine du Plessix. *Soviet Women*. New York: Doubleday, 1989.
A revealing and readable book about contemporary women—their lives, work, thoughts, and feelings—by an American writer of Russian descent.

Hingley, Ronald. *The Russian Mind*. New York: Charles Scribner's Sons, 1977.
A study of Russian behavior with numerous examples from history and literature, by an English scholar and translator with a great sense of humor.

Kohn, Hans. "Russia: The Permanent Mission." Chap. 7 in *The Twentieth Century*. New York: MacMillan, 1949.
Russia's relationship to Europe and the rest of the world, as seen by the foremost historian of modern nationalism.

Kohn, Hans, ed. *The Mind of Modern Russia*. New Brunswick, NJ: Rutgers University Press, 1955.
Selected readings from great Russian writers and thinkers.

Laqueur, Walter. *The Long Road to Freedom, Russia and Glasnost*. New York: MacMillan, Collier Books, 1989.
A penetrating analysis of glasnost based on Russia's past and present, by a renowned historian.

Mehnert, Klaus. *The Russians and Their Favorite Books.* Stanford, CA: Hoover Institution Press, 1983.
The concerns and interests of the Russian people, as seen through their most popular authors and most frequently read novels, by a German who was born in Moscow and worked there for many years as a foreign correspondent.

Noble, John, and John King. *USSR, A Travel Survival Kit.* Berkeley: Lonely Planet Publications, 1991.
Everything a traveler needs to know.

Rand, Robert. *Comrade Lawyer, Inside Soviet Justice in an Era of Reform.* Boulder: Westview Press, 1991.
A study of the Soviet legal system and the day-to-day work of defense counsels, by a Russian-speaking American lawyer.

Riasanovsky, Nicholas V. *A History of Russia,* 5th ed. New York: Oxford University Press, 1992.
A widely used college text by a University of California professor.

Ripp, Victor. *Pizza in Pushkin Square, What Russians Think About Americans and the American Way of Life.* New York: Simon and Schuster, 1990.
An American of Russian descent visits Russia, relates his encounters with Russians, examines their perceptions about America, and provides insights on both American and Russian behavior.

Smith, Hedrick. *The New Russians.* New York: Avon Books, 1991.
An updated version of the 1990 book on change in the Soviet Union, by a former *New York Times* correspondent in Moscow.

Starr, S. Frederick. "Reform in Russia: A Peculiar Pattern." *Wilson Quarterly* (Spring 1989), 37-50.
The similarities between Mr. Gorbachev's reforms and previous efforts at reform in Russian history, by a noted scholar of Russian culture.

Stites, Richard. *Revolutionary Dreams, Utopian Vision and Experimental Life in the Russian Revolution*. New York: Oxford University Press, 1989.

The dreams of Russian utopian thinkers, drawn from native Russian traditions, and how they were shattered in the Stalinist era. By a professor of history at Georgetown University.

Szamuely, Tibor. *The Russian Tradition*. New York: McGraw-Hill, 1974.

How history has shaped the Russians and produced absolutism of rule, both in the established order as well as in the revolutionary tradition which opposed it. By a Hungarian-born scholar who lived and studied in both Russia and England.

Vakar, Nicholas P. *The Taproot of Soviet Society*. New York: Harper and Brothers, 1962.

An analysis of Soviet society and its roots in the Russian peasant past, by a professor of Russian civilization at Wheaton College, Massachusetts.

Young, Cathy. *Growing Up in Moscow, Memories of a Soviet Girlhood*. New York: Ticknor and Fields, 1989.

A former Russian schoolgirl now living in the United States describes her schooling and everyday life in the 1970s.

Index